Unleavened

The Ultimate Pesach Cookbook

Ashira Ungar

Featuring Photography by:
Eliyahu Ungar-Sargon

Unleavened

The Ultimate Pesach Cookbook

Ashira Ungar

Featuring Photography by:
Eliyahu Ungar-Sargon

Table of Contents

Entrees 92

Quinoa Bowls 132

Sauces & Staples 140

Accompaniments   **154**

Sweets   **174**

Index   **210**

Acknowledgements

First and foremost, I have to thank my husband. Without the yeoman's effort he put in to create the magnificent photography in this book, the project would not exist.

Michal, Grey and Noa...our fellow Fineschmeckers...thank-you for letting me use your kitchen for some of the testing and photography! Your inexhaustable love and generosity know no bounds.

Amira and Jonathan...thank-you for your constant love and support.

To my "no-longer-in-Chicago" peeps...Nicole, Ken, Shim, Leah and Anna...and my "no-longer-in-LA" family in Paris...David, Vanessa and Judith...I am so grateful for you.

To Rabbi Lopatin, who taught me the value of simcha in Yiddishkeit, thank-you for everything.

Aaron, you've been a life-saver more times than I can count.

To Mom, who taught me how to cook and set the highest expectations imaginable with her many Liisa-extravaganzas...kiitos paljon.

Thank-you to everyone in Eliyahu's family, (too numerous to list by name) who have become my nearest and dearest over the years.

Josh Lobell, thank-you for being one of my biggest food cheerleaders. You always make me feel like a proper chef.

To all of my guinea pigs who have tasted these recipes along the way, and all the people I've had the privilege of hosting over the years...there is nothing I love more than having you over for Shabbos.

Dedication

This book is dedicated in loving memory of

Rebbetzin Racheil Gettinger a'h
and
Wilhelm Ungar zt'l

Introduction

Another macaroon. I sat in my apartment staring at the container of cloyingly sweet, yet oddly dry confections feeling sick. "It doesn't matter how hungry I am," I said to myself. "There is no way I can choke down another macaroon."

This was my first experience of trying to keep some semblance of kosher for Pesach. At the time, I had no rabbi or community and few resources...simply an intuition that this was something I wanted to try my best to observe. In the very limited kosher section at my grocery store, the only items I could find that had a "Kosher for Passover" label were macaroons. So that's all I bought. And I tried to live on them for days. Clearly, this was not the best introduction to Pesach cuisine.

Over the years, I continued to have a fraught relationship with the holiday. I came to learn the importance of simcha during chaggim, yet the food at Pesach always cast a pall for me. The effort it takes to prepare a home for the holiday is epic. The boisterous joy of the meals goes down in family lore. But the actual food is often the low point. Most of the people I know think of Pesach food as tolerable, at best.

This disconnect between the importance and joy of yontef and the misery of the gastronomical experience led me down a three year path of exploration. Part of the reason Pesach was challenging for me was because I didn't grow up with family traditions. I finally decided to embrace this as a strength rather than a weakness. My lack of experience freed me from the constraints of what was usually done and allowed me to develop a totally fresh perspective.

I always tell people that I think Pesach cuisine should be the most delicious food we eat all year. This cookbook is an attempt to make that vision a reality.

Pesach

Pesach (Passover) is a Jewish holiday that commemorates the Israelite exodus from slavery in Egypt. G-d brought ten plagues upon the Egyptians which culminated in the death of every firstborn male. However, Moses instructed the children of Israel to put the blood of a lamb on their doorposts so that the angel of death would pass over them. Through a series of miracles, the Israelites were set free and escaped from Egypt. A full explanation of the history, laws and customs of Pesach is beyond the scope of this book. If you are interested in learning more about the holiday, consult a local Rabbi.

The holiday lasts for 8 days (7 in Israel), but the preparations begin much earlier. Since the Israelites had to flee quickly, there was no time for the bread to rise. Therefore, they only brought unleavened bread on the journey. Observant Jews not only refrain from eating all leavened food items (Chametz) during Pesach, but they also remove all traces of Chametz from their homes, kasher their kitchens again, and switch out all of the dishes and kitchen utensils. Over the years, different Jewish communities have developed different customs about which foods are prohibited over the holiday. For Ashkenazi Jews, this includes a category called "kitniyot" which comprises legumes (and MANY great spices!) among other things.

During the first two nights of Pesach (one night in Israel), families gather to enjoy a festive ritual meal called a seder. The story of Passover is retold while reading through a text called the Haggadah. In addition to four cups of wine (plus a large cup for the prophet Elijah) and a lot of matzah, there is a seder plate which features foods that represent different elements of the story of the exodus.

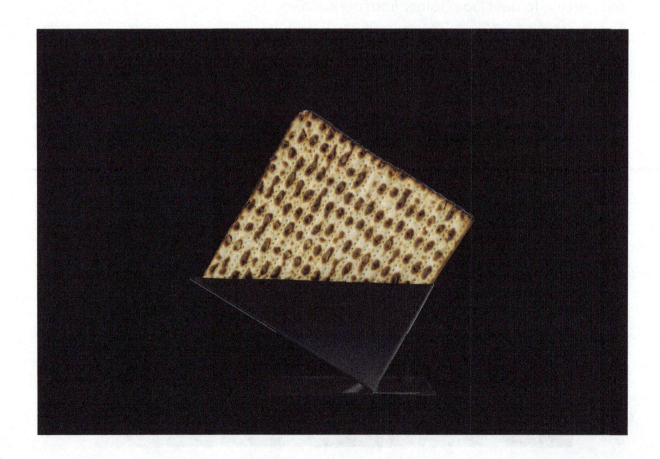

Seder Plate

There are six* items that are tradionally put on a seder plate. However, different families have their own customs about which foods represent some of these.

Zero'a: shank bone
Beitzah: egg (hard boiled, then burned)
Maror: bitter herbs, often horseradish
Charoset: a paste of fruit, nuts, wine and cinnamon
Karpas: parsley, celery or boiled potatoes
Chazeret: vegetable, often romaine lettuce

Additionally, salt water for dipping

*some seder plates have five items, omitting Chazeret

Dips and "Bready" Delights

Pesach Bread (or Loaf)

The dream of baking something that I could use to approximate a sandwich over Pesach is what launched my deep dive into chametz-free cuisine. I know people who don't even like to use the term "bread" over the holiday, so I also call this "Pesach Loaf." Out of an abundance of caution, I consulted with multiple rabbeim about whether this recipe was acceptable, and without exeption I was given their blessings.

I always use a bread pan that is 8x4x2" when I make Pesach Bread. The small pan allows the bread to rise more and creates a better result for sandwiches, etc. I have tried making it in larger pans, but the loaves can be a bit flat when the batter spreads more.

Ingredients:

1 cup Almond Butter
4 Eggs, lightly beaten
1 Tbs. Apple Cider Vinegar
1 Tbs. Lemon Juice
1 tsp. Honey
½ tsp. Salt
1 tsp. Baking Soda

Non-Stick Cooking Spray

Instructions:

Preheat oven to 350°F.

Combine almond butter and eggs in a medium bowl and mix well. Add remaining ingredients. Mix until the batter is smooth.

Coat a small bread pan with non-stick cooking spray and pour batter into pan.

Bake for 35-40 minutes. Allow to cool before slicing.

Pesach Laffa

There are a lot of ways to use this recipe. The "laffas" work well as sandwich wraps, they go well with dips or spreads, and they can be cut into wedges and toasted or baked and used like pita chips. If you prefer a slightly thicker texture, don't allow the batter to spread out too much in the pan. For a thinner version, allow it to spread out a bit more in the pan or add 1 extra egg white to thin the batter.

Ingredients:

2 cups Tapioca Flour
2 cups Almond Flour
2 Eggs, lightly beaten
1 cup Water
2 tsp. White Vinegar
¾ - 1 tsp. Salt
2 tsp. Baking Soda
½ tsp. Garlic Powder
½ tsp. Onion Powder

Non-Stick Cooking Spray or Oil for frying

Instructions:

Combine tapioca and almond flours in a mixing bowl. Mix with a whisk or fork to eliminate lumps.

Add remainder of ingredients (except the oil for frying) and mix well into a smooth batter.

Heat a skillet over medium heat. Grease the pan with non-stick cooking spray or a dash of cooking oil. Once the pan is hot, add batter. ½ cup of batter will yield a roughly 6-7 inch laffa, and 1 cup of batter will yield a roughly 9-10 inch laffa. For a thicker laffa, do not allow the batter to spread out too much. Once bubbles form on the surface and the batter is no longer runny, flip to cook on the other side until golden brown.

If you are using the laffas to make wraps, it is easiest to fold them into thirds on a cooling rack once you remove them from the pan. This will allow them to keep the right shape as they cool and they will be much easier to work with.

Yields approximately 6 large (10") laffas.

Bean-Free Pesach Hummous

Hummous is a staple of my household, so it's one of those things that everyone misses on Pesach. So when I finally got this recipe to work, it was a massive achievement. I usually serve this with vegetable crudite and pesach laffa, but it even makes matzah delicious.

Ingredients:

1 cup Raw Cashews
Water for soaking (approximately
    1 ½ -2 cups)
4 tsp. Lemon Juice
2 cloves Garlic
3 Tbs. Olive Oil
1 Tbs. Quinoa Flour*
1 Tbs. Hazelnut Butter
½ tsp. Salt

Instructions:

Place cashews in a bowl with 1 clove of crushed garlic. Pour water over the cashews and garlic and mix gently. Set aside, and soak for about 4 hours. (If you are short on time, you can use boiling water and soak for 1 hour.)

After the cashews and garlic have soaked, remove them, but reserve the liquid. Place cashews and the garlic from the liquid into a food processor. Add the additional garlic clove (minced), lemon juice, olive oil, hazelnut butter, quinoa flour and salt. Add 3-4 tablespoons of the reserved soaking liquid. Blend until you reach a smooth texture that looks like hummous.

Adjust lemon, oil, salt and garlic to taste. Use additional soaking liquid if you'd like to thin it out a bit.

*If you cannot find quinoa flour, you can make it at home. You essentially just need to blend dry quinoa to a fine powder. If you have the time, there are a few extra steps you can take. For the best possible version, (if your quinoa is not pre-rinsed) start by rinsing under cold water and lay it out on a flat surface until it is dry. Once it is dry, toast it gently on the stove over a low heat with no oil in the pan. Toss and stir frequently so that the quinoa doesn't burn or stick to the pan. Allow to cool completely before blending. Blend in a spice mill, food processor or blender until you have a fine powder. Pass the powder through a strainer to eliminate any large clumps. Store in an airtight container.

Serves 4-6

Roasted Carrot Hummous

I love to make spreads and dips for Pesach because they play well with so many foods. There is always so much extra matzah, and these kinds of spreads are a great way to make it more interesting. You can also serve them with vegetable crudité, chips or Pesach Laffa (page 18). When I first developed this recipe, I wanted to include a bit of hazelnut butter. I've omitted it here, because it threw off the balance, and the spread is really better when the pure flavor of the roasted carrot comes through...but if you'd like to try a variation, add a bit of hazelnut butter and judge for yourself.

Ingredients:

2 ¾ cups Carrots, peeled and
    chopped
5 Tbs. Olive Oil, divided
Salt and Pepper to taste
4 cloves Garlic, roasted
2 tsp. Lemon Juice

Instructions:

Preheat oven to 400°F.

Toss the peeled and chopped carrots with 2 tsp. olive oil and a sprinkle of salt and pepper. Spread them out onto a parchment lined baking sheet and bake for about 1 hour, stirring occasionally. They should be soft and a bit browned.

To roast the garlic, rub off any loose skin from the bulb. Carefully slice off the top (pointed) end of the bulb. Each clove should be exposed. Use a small knife to cut off the tips of any cloves that are still encased. Place the garlic in a small baking dish or simply wrap it in foil. (I always just wrap the garlic in some foil. It is the easiest way to roast.) Drizzle with about 1 tsp. olive oil and sprinkle with salt and pepper. Cover the dish with foil and roast in a 400°F oven for 30-35 minutes. This can be done while the carrots are roasting in the same oven. Save the extra roasted garlic for use as a spread or add it to any dish that calls for garlic. It is especially good on baked or mashed potatoes.

Once the carrots and garlic are roasted, place carrots, 4 cloves of the garlic, 4 tablespoons of olive oil, 2 teaspoons of lemon juice and about 1/8 teaspoon salt into the bowl of a food processor. Blend until smooth.

Adjust lemon and salt to taste.

Serves 4-6

Baba Ghanoush

Baba Ghanoush is one of my favorite foods. The version I usually find in kosher markets is not authentic. They are usually mayonnaise based, creamy dips that are a far cry from the real thing. Since real baba ghanoush is made with tahina paste, which is kitniyot, I didn't think of it as an option for Pesach...until I discovered the joy of Hazelnut butter. Obviously, the flavor of hazelnut is not the same as tahina, but in this dish it gives a surprisingly similar vibe. As with all recipes based on roasted eggplant, it is difficult to give specific amounts. The size and amount of roasted eggplant flesh that you will get is highly variable, so use these amounts as a guide, and adjust ingredients to your taste.

Ingredients:

2 large Eggplants, about 2 cups roasted
2 Tbs. Hazelnut Butter
1 clove Garlic, minced (a little goes a long way in this recipe, start small because you can always add more.)
1 Tbs. Olive Oil
1 Tbs. Lemon Juice
½ tsp. Salt

Instructions:

Roast the eggplants. This can be done in a 400°F oven for about 1 hour, under a high broiler or over a flame on the stove or grill. Start by poking holes in the eggplants with a small paring knife. This allows the heat to escape. If you forget this step, there is a good chance they will explode and make a mess of your oven! If roasting in the oven or broiler, line the pan with foil because they get messy as they roast. Check frequently and turn or rotate as needed. Roast until the eggplants collapse and are charred/smoky and soft.

Allow the eggplants to cool a bit before working with them. Cut open each one and scoop out the flesh into a mixing bowl. Use a fork and/or a small paring knife to chop up the flesh so that there are no overly large pieces.

Add all remaining ingredients to the bowl and mix thoroughly.

Adjust seasoning to taste.

Optional: top with pomegranate seeds

Serve with vegetables, chips, Pesach Laffa or matzah.

Serves 4-6

Aubergine Dip

I lived in England for a few years, so I got in the habit of referring to eggplant as "aubergine." When I added this recipe to my every-week go-to list, I was still in that mindset, so I listed it as "Aubergine Dip." It still lives by that name in our family. This is one of my absolute favorite things and I make it all the time. It is part of the appetizer course for almost every dairy meal, and it's a great staple to keep in the fridge for dipping vegetables. The non-pesach version calls for cumin, so if you make it during the year, be sure to add cumin to taste. This is also one of those recipes that is hard to write because eggplants vary in size and the amount that you get after roasting is variable based on a number of factors. I'm listing the rough amounts for each ingredient, but this is one of those recipes that will be best if you adjust amounts according to your taste as you go.

Ingredients:

2 Large Eggplants (about 2 cups after roasting)
1 - 1½ Tbs. Olive Oil
1½ Tbs. Lemon Juice
Salt, to taste (around ½ tsp.)
Black Pepper, to taste (around ¼ tsp.)
1 clove Garlic, crushed
⅓ cup Walnuts, chopped
¼ - ⅓ cup Leben (or Greek Yogurt)
2-3 oz. Feta Cheese, crumbled

Instructions:

Roast the eggplants. This can be done in a 400°F oven for about 1 hour, under a high broiler or over a flame on the stove or grill. Start by poking holes in the eggplants with a small paring knife. This allows the heat to escape. If you forget this step, there is a good chance they will explode and make a mess of your oven! If roasting in the oven or broiler, line the pan with foil because they get messy as they roast. Check frequently and turn or rotate as needed. Roast until the eggplants collapse and are charred/smoky and soft.

Allow the eggplants to cool a bit before working with them. Cut open each one and scoop out the flesh into a mixing bowl. Use a fork and/or a small paring knife to chop up the flesh so that there are no overly large pieces.

Add olive oil, lemon juice, salt and pepper to the eggplant and mix well. Adjust these to taste before proceeding.

Add garlic and walnuts. Mix well. Adjust to taste.

Add leben and feta and mix well. Adjust to taste.

Chill and serve as a dip with vegetables, chips, Pesach Laffa or matzah.

Serves 4-6

Matboucha

Matboucha is a grilled vegetable "salad" that's really more of a dip. It's great with terra chips, pesach laffa, or vegetable crudité...or as a side with any dish that needs a little something extra. You can add extra cayenne to make it spicier, but even without the added heat, it has a lot of flavor. It does take some time to make this dish, but it really is worth it! I almost always double the recipe when I make this because it is so time consuming. It's easier to do two batches at once rather than make it twice. And people always want more, so it never goes to waste.

Ingredients:

4-5 very ripe Tomatoes
4 Red Bell Peppers
4 Poblano Peppers
8-10 cloves Garlic, minced
½ cup Oil
1 Tbs. Paprika
¼ - ½ tsp. Cayenne (or more to taste)
pinch Sugar
1 Tbs. Tomato Paste
1 tsp. Salt (or a bit less, to taste)

Instructions:

Roast the red bell peppers and the poblanos. This can either be done in a 450°-500°F oven, under the broiler or over an open flame on the stove. Before roasting, poke holes in the peppers with a small knife so that they will not explode while cooking. Roast until the peppers are completely soft and a bit charred, turning as needed.

After roasting, place them in a zip top plastic bag or seal in a foil pouch to cool. Allowing the peppers to cool in a closed container will allow them to steam a bit and this will make it easier to peel off the skin.

Once the peppers have cooled completely, peel off the skin, remove the seeds and stems and chop them finely. Set aside.

While the peppers are roasting, peel seed and chop the tomatoes. This is easiest if you par boil them first. To do this, boil a pot of water on the stove. Use a small knife to cut a shallow "X" into the bottom of each tomato. Place tomatoes into the boiling water and cook for about 30-60 seconds. (You will see the skin at the edges of the "X" start to pull back.) Remove tomatoes from water and peel them. Remove the seeds and chop finely. Set aside.

In a saucepan on the stove, cook the peeled/chopped tomatoes over medium heat. Do not add oil to the pan. Cook for 5-10 minutes, stirring frequently.

Add all of the remaining ingredients except tomato paste. Cook for 2 hours over a low heat, stirring as needed.

Add tomato paste. Cook for another 30 minutes. The matboucha is ready when it looks shiny and thick.

Adjust seasoning to taste.

Serves 6-8

Brazilian Cheesy Bites

These "bready" bites are a bit like popovers. They are one of my favorite dishes to make every Pesach, and I've learned a lot from mistakes I've made over the years. The first thing to note is that these require a bit of specialized equipment, but they are worth the investment! You will need a dairy non-stick, metal cupcake/muffin pan and a dairy food processor or blender. These don't have to be expensive. I bought a cheap muffin pan for about $12 and a mini food processor for around $35 and they worked great. And, if you pack them away to be part of your Pesach cookware, it's a one-time investment. When I tried to make them with a disposable muffin tin, they did not rise at all. For some reason, they need the smooth sides of a proper pan to grip. Also, when I did not fill the cups nearly to the top, they also failed to develop the correct airy texture. They still taste great, but for the best result, you'll need to use the right kind of pan and fill the cups almost to the top.

Ingredients:

2 eggs
2/3 cup Olive Oil
1 1/3 cup 2% Milk
3 cups Tapioca Flour
1 cup grated Mozzarella Cheese (packed)
1½ tsp. Salt
Cooking Spray or Oil for pan

Instructions:

Preheat oven to 400° F.

Lightly beat the egg, and combine with olive oil and milk. Mix in tapioca flour and salt. Add cheese and mix well.

Once all of the ingredients are combined, transfer mixture to a food processor or blender. (This can be done in batches in a mini food processor.) Blend until the mixture is smooth.

Before pouring batter into pan, spray each cup with cooking spray or coat with olive oil. Do NOT use cupcake liners…they stick to the dough and ruin the end result. If the cups in the pan are greased well, the Cheesy Bites will pop right out.

Pour batter into pan, nearly to the top of each cup. (no more than 1/8 inch from the top.) When I left too much room at the top (about ¼ inch… they did not "pop").

Bake for 22-25 minutes until the Cheesy Bites are golden brown and pop up over the edges of the pan.

Yields approximately 15 muffins

Pesach Pancakes

These pancakes are always a hit when I make them for people. So much so, that they really have become a year-round low-carb staple. They are so good that you might not even feel the need to drown them in maple syrup. I have found that the availability of almond flour varies between different kosher markets during Pesach. There are very finely ground, sifted almond flours available in some places, while others only offer coarser grinds. (Often called simply "ground almonds.") I've made this recipe with both types...and the good news is, they both work! But the results are a bit different. The batter made with a very fine almond flour is a bit "wetter" and the texture of the pancakes is more even. You may want to add an extra 1-2 Tablespoons of almond flour if you have a very finely ground almond flour and you want a slightly drier batter. These pancakes are also a bit more delicate to cook than regular pancakes, so it is easier to make smaller cakes and let them cook most of the way through before flipping them very carefully.

Ingredients:

1⅛ cup Almond Flour (for very fine almond flour, add 1-2 extra Tablespoons if you want a drier batter.)
¼ tsp. Baking Soda
¼ tsp. Salt
2 Eggs, lightly beaten
2 Tbs. Oil
2 Tbs. 2% Milk
1-2 Tbs. Honey, depending on desired sweetness
1 tsp. White Vinegar

Instructions:

In a large bowl, combine almond flour, baking soda, and salt and mix well.

In a small bowl, lightly beat eggs. Add oil, milk, honey and vinegar and whisk together.

Add the egg mixture to the almond flour mixture and combine thoroughly.

Heat butter or oil in a skillet. Pour batter into pan and cook in batches. It is easiest to make 4 small pancakes or 2 medium pancakes per batch, since the pancakes are a bit fragile. Cook thoroughly on the first side before flipping to cook the other side.

Serve with maple syrup or jam if desired.

Serves 4

Pizza Crust

I feel like everyone has a version of pizza for Pesach. I was so excited the first time I was told about Matzah Pizza...but I was met with a piece of matzah with some ketchup and cheese that broke my heart. Since then, I've had dozens of increasingly elaborate versions of matzah pizza that always leave me underwhelmed. Pizza is very difficult to execute at home because without a specialized pizza oven that can reach very high temperatures, it will almost never be as good as something prepared in a restaurant. However, for a homemade option, this crust works well. It can also be used as a base for a variety of flatbreads.

Ingredients:

½ cup Water
¼ cup Olive Oil
1 Egg
¾ cup Tapioca Flour
¾ cup Almond Flour (use an almond flour that is as finely ground as possible)
½ tsp. Salt
¼ tsp. Garlic
¼ tsp Basil
¼ tsp Oregano
¼ cup Parmesan, grated

Instructions:

Preheat oven to 375°F.

Combine tapioca flour, almond flour, spices and grated parmesan in a bowl and mix thoroughly. Set aside.

Lightly beat the egg. Whisk in the water and olive oil and mix until well combined. Add this liquid mixture into the dry mixture. Mix until a cohesive batter forms.

Line a baking sheet with foil and parchment paper. Pour the batter onto the sheet and spread into the desired shape. This recipe tends to work best as a rectangle. The batter is very runny, so just spread it out onto the baking sheet and shape it as well as you can.

Bake for 25-30 minutes.

Remove from the oven and raise the temperature to 400°F. Top with tomato sauce, mozzarella and any other desired pizza toppings and return to oven for another 8-10 minutes. You may also put it under a broiler for the last minute or two to brown the cheese.

Note: This crust also works as a great substitute for flatbread. Top with goat cheese, fig, arugula, pistachios and a balsamic glaze...or whatever your favorite flatbread topping is.

Yields 1 (8-10") crust

Pesach Crepes

This is a versatile dish that can be savory or sweet. Filled with mushrooms, spinach, cheese and pesto, it can be a main course. Filled with fruit or chocolate spread, it can be a beautiful dessert. There are really no limits to the number of ways you can use this recipe to enhance you Pesach meals.

Ingredients:

2 Eggs, lightly beaten
2 Tbs. Water
½ cup Tapioca Flour
pinch of Salt, to taste
Oil or Cooking Spray

Instructions:

Lightly beat the eggs in a mixing bowl. Add water, tapioca flour and salt and mix thoroughly. Set aside while the pan heats up.

On the stove, heat a small skillet pan over medium heat. Grease the pan with a bit of oil or non-stick cooking spray. Pour batter into the pan and cook for 1-3 minutes per side.

Serve warm, with either sweet or savory fillings.

Yields 3-4 crepes

Soups

Wild Mushroom Soup

This is a hearty soup that is almost a meal in itself. If you cannot locate dried porcini mushrooms in your area, you can get fresh porcinis and dry them on your own. It may seem like a hassle to track down such a variety of mushrooms, but this absolutely delicious soup is worth the effort.

Ingredients:

- 1 oz. Dried Porcini Mushrooms
- 2 Tbs. Olive Oil
- 2 Tbs. Margarine
- 2 Leeks, thinly sliced (white parts only)
- 2 Shallots, chopped
- 3 Cloves Garlic, minced
- 4 oz. Fresh Shiitake Mushrooms, chopped
- 4 oz. Fresh Brown Clamshell Mushrooms, chopped
- 4 oz. Royal Trumpet Mushrooms
- 6 cups Vegetable Stock
- ½ cup Coconut Cream
- 1 tsp. Dried Thyme
- Salt and Pepper to taste

Instructions:

Place the dried porcinis in a bowl with 1 cup of warm water. Set aside and allow to soak for about 1 hour. Do not discard the soaking liquid.

Heat oil and margarine or butter in a large pot on the stove. Add the leeks and shallots and cook for 5-7 minutes. Add garlic and cook for another 2-3 minutes.

Add the chopped fresh mushrooms to the pan and cook for 5-8 minutes until they soften and release their juices.

Add stock, thyme, salt and pepper and bring to a boil. (I use about ½ tsp. of salt at this stage, then add more at the end, as needed.)

Remove the porcinis from the soaking liquid. Add the liquid to the soup. Chop the rehydrated mushrooms and add them to the soup. Simmer for about 30 minutes.

Remove soup from heat. Transfer the soup in batches to a blender, or use an immersion blender, and puree until smooth.

Return the soup to the stove. Add coconut cream and heat through. Adjust seasoning to taste.

Serves 6-8

Garlic Soup

This is my husband's favorite soup. Every time I have asked him what soup he'd like...this is, without fail, his answer. The concept of garlic soup might sound strange, but it is absolutely delicious. The key to this dish is slicing the garlic paper thin. It takes a lot of work if you use a knife...but it is possible! I did it for years before I found a tool specially designed to slice garlic. I now make this much more frequently.

Ingredients:

4 cups Water
2 Tbs. Olive Oil
2 large bulbs of Garlic, broken
  into cloves, peeled and sliced
  as thinly as possible
3-4 oz. Feta Cheese, crumbled
1 cup Labane (or Greek Yogurt)
Salt and Pepper to taste

Instructions:

In a saucepan, over medium heat, bring water and oil to a boil.

Add sliced garlic and a pinch of salt. Reduce heat and simmer for at least 45-60 minutes. Add a bit of water if the level has reduced significantly.

Add feta and labane and stir over a low heat for 3-5 minutes. Do not allow to boil. Adjust salt and pepper to taste.

Serve warm.

Serves 4-6

French Onion Soup

After making this soup for years, I have learned that the key to a really amazing French Onion Soup is simply time. You have to cook the onions long enough to develop a rich, dark, mahogany color. I have tasted many mediocre versions…and I can always tell just by looking at the color whether the onions were not cooked long enough. The other important thing is to be very careful not to let the onions burn. If they burn at all, the smoky flavor will ruin the dish.

Ingredients:

4 large Yellow or White Onions, thinly sliced
2 Tbs. Olive Oil
2 Tbs. Butter or Margarine*
4 cups Vegetable or Beef stock*
Salt and Pepper to taste

Instructions:

Heat oil and butter (or margarine) in a large soup pot. Add onions. Sautee the onions until they are a rich brown (mahogany) color. (approximately 1 hour 30 minutes)

Once the onions start to darken, stir frequently. Do not allow onions to stick to the bottom of the pan. Do not allow the onions to burn at all.

Only after the onions are a rich mahogany color, add stock. Mix well. Simmer for 20-30 minutes.

Add salt and pepper to taste.

Optional: Garnish soup with Swiss, Mozzerella or Gruyere cheese (if serving at a dairy meal).

*This soup can be meat, dairy or parve depending on what kind of stock you use, and whether you use margarine or butter.

Serves 4

Broccoli Cauliflower Soup

This is one of my favorite soups. It is unapologetically dairy, but it is totally worth it. Dairy meals can be sophisticated, delicious and substantial, and I always encourage people to consider eating meat-free more often.

Ingredients:

2 Tbs. Olive Oil
1 Red Onion, diced
3 Cloves Garlic, minced
10 oz. Broccoli Florets
10 oz. Cauliflower, chopped
1 Tbs. Potato Starch
2 ½ cups Milk
1 ½ cups Vegetable Stock
½ cup Swiss Cheese, shredded
¾ cup Sour Cream
2 tsp. Paprika
Salt to taste

Instructions:

Sautee the onion in the olive oil in a large pot over medium heat for about 7-10 minutes.

Once it begins to caramelize, add garlic, broccoli and cauliflower. Cook for another 5 minutes, stirring constantly.

Add potato starch, mix well.

Add the milk and stock, and bring to a boil. Reduce heat and simmer for 30 minutes.

Remove the pot from heat and blend the soup until smooth. It is easiest to do this with an immersion blender, but the soup can be blended in batches in a food processor or blender and returned to the pot.

Return the soup to the stove and add cheese, sour cream, paprika and salt.

Heat through until the cheese melts, but don't allow the soup to boil.

Serve Hot.

Serves 4-6

Sweet And Sour Cabbage Soup

I created this soup based on the cabbage filling I make for a savory Finnish pastry called Kaalipiirakka. Most traditional Finnish recipes go something like this: "add enough of this and enough of that, cook in a medium oven til done." Therefore, I don't have actual amounts for the cabbage filling…I always make it to taste. For this soup, I have a guideline for the amounts of honey and vinegar that should work well, but like any good Finnish recipe, you should adjust these ingredients to your taste. Especially since "1 head of cabbage" will vary in size, feel free to add more/less vinegar and honey until you find the right balance for you.

Ingredients:

2 Tbs. Olive Oil
2 Tbs. Margarine or Butter*
1 head of Cabbage, chopped (I generally use white cabbage, but red will work)
2 Shallots, sliced
5 Tbs. White Vinegar
2 Tbs. Honey
4 cups Vegetable Broth
1 tsp. Tomato Paste
Salt to taste (about ¾ -1 tsp.)
Black Pepper to taste (start with about ¼ tsp and add as needed.)

Instructions:

Heat 2 Tbs. olive oil in a large pot over medium high heat. Add shallots and sauté for about 5-10 minutes.

Add 2 Tbs. margarine (or butter) and the cabbage. Cook for about 20 minutes, stirring occasionally so that the cabbage does not burn.

Add vinegar, honey and ½ tsp. salt. Mix well and cook for another 30 minutes, until the cabbage is a deep golden color.

Add tomato paste and broth. Bring to simmer and cook for 15-20 minutes to allow the flavor to develop.

Add salt and pepper to taste.

Adjust vinegar and honey to taste.

Serve hot.

*Be sure to use margarine if you are making this parve.

Serves 6-8

Karelian Borscht

This is an old family recipe from eastern Finland. It can work as a parve vegetarian soup course as part of a meal, or you can add pre-cooked sausages and serve it as a main course. Great sausage really makes this dish, so I highly recommend the meaty version.

Ingredients:

4 medium Beets, peeled and grated
2 Tbs. Olive Oil
1 tsp. Salt, plus more to taste
4 Tbs. Potato Starch
2 Tbs. White Vinegar
1 Tbs. Balsamic Vinegar
1 small head Red Cabbage, shredded
3 cloves Garlic, minced
2 Carrots, peeled and grated
1 Tbs. Honey
8 cups Broth

Instructions:

In a large pot, sauté beets in olive oil until soft. Add salt, potato starch and vinegar and mix well. Cook for another 3-5 minutes.

Add cabbage, garlic, carrots, honey and broth. Bring to a boil. Reduce heat to a simmer and cook for at least 3 hours. (Add water as needed as stew reduces in volume.)

If using sausage, cut into roughly ½" slices and add to the stew. Heat through.

Adjust seasoning to taste. Add additional vinegar or honey to taste. Serve warm.

Optional: 1 lb. Pre-Cooked Sausage

Serves 6

Gazpacho

The single most important element in a great gazpacho is bread. So why on earth would I include it as a Pesach dish? I nearly gave up on this recipe because I felt like I couldn't come up with a bread-less version that felt true to the spirit of the original. When I finally landed on using pine nuts in the soup, it changed everything. The nuts give this gazpacho a texture and flavor that are really special. And the kiwi adds a bit of sweetness with a twist. This is a great soup for Shabbos because it can be made in advance and it gets better with time as it sits overnight.

Ingredients:

3 large ripe Tomatoes (about 2½ cups)
⅔ cup Yellow Onion, chopped
2 cloves Garlic, minced
1 large English Cucumber, peeled, seeded and roughly chopped (about 1½ cups)
1 Red Bell Pepper, seeded and roughly chopped (about 1¼ cups)
1 Kiwi, peeled and roughly chopped
⅓ cup Pine Nuts
1 Tbs. Cooking Sherry
2 Tbs. Balsamic Vinegar
1 Tbs. Olive Oil
Salt and Pepper, to taste

Instructions:

Add all ingredients to a food processor and puree until very smooth. This can take 2-3 minutes.

Adjust seasoning to taste. This recipe needs a fair amount of salt, so continue adding until the flavor of the vegetables really comes through.

Cover and refrigerate until ready to serve.

Serve chilled.

Thin out with water, if necessary, to reach desired consistency.

Serves 4-6

Carrot Ginger Soup

This is a delicious soup that I make often during the year. It usually calls for cumin and coriander, so I had to make a few changes for Pesach. The thing I love most about this soup is the spiciness of the fresh ginger. It's a great way to add some interesting flavors to a meal.

Ingredients:

2 Tbs. Olive Oil
1 large Onion, chopped
2 cloves, Garlic, minced
¼ cup (Packed) Fresh Ginger, minced
1 lb. Carrots (about 14oz. after peeling) peeled and chopped
4 cups Broth
1 Tbs. Honey
½ cup Coconut Milk
½ tsp. Allspice
Salt and Black Pepper, to taste

Instructions:

In a large pot, heat olive oil over a medium high heat.

Add onion and cook for 10-12 minutes, until a bit caramelized.

Add garlic and cook for 3-5 minutes.

Add carrots and ginger and cook for 8-10 minutes, stirring frequently.

Add broth and bring to a boil. Reduce heat a bit and cook for about 30-45 minutes.

Remove the soup from the heat. Use an immersion blender to blend, or transfer in batches to a blender or food processor. Make sure that the soup is thoroughly blended and totally smooth. Return to pot (if you didn't use an immersion blender), and return the pot to the stove.

Add honey, coconut milk, allspice, salt and pepper. Mix well and heat through. Adjust seasoning to taste.

Serves 4-6

Salads

Carrot Hazelnut Salad

PARVE

This is a very simple, light salad. It is important to grate the carrots yourself. I've made it in the past using pre-shredded carrots, but they are a bit too big and very dry. Grating them just before making the salad ensures the right texture.

Ingredients:

2 medium Carrots, peeled and
    grated/shredded
3 Tbs. Ground Roasted Hazelnuts*
3 Tbs. Cilantro, chopped
1-1½ Tbs. Lime Juice (start with
    1 Tbs. and add more to taste)
Cayenne Pepper to taste
Salt to taste

Instructions:

Combine all ingredients in a bowl and mix thoroughly.

Adjust seasoning to taste. You may also need to add more cilantro, hazelnuts or lime juice based on your taste.

*Grind hazelnuts into a rough powder in a small food processor or nut grinder. Do not over blend or they will turn into hazelnut butter. After grinding, measure out 3 tablespoons.

Serves 4

Spinach Salad

Spinach is healthy, and this is a delicious way to incorporate it into your meal. This salad is easy to prepare, but don't dress it until just before serving to prevent excess wilting.

Ingredients:

8-10 cups Baby Spinach, roughly chopped
2 cups Cherry Tomatoes, cut into halves or quarters
1 can Artichoke hearts, chopped (Substitute hearts of palm if unavailable during Pesach)
1 Avocado, diced
½ cup Walnuts, chopped
1-2 Tbs. Olive Oil
1 Tbs. Balsamic Vinegar
Salt and Pepper, to taste

Optional: Add a pinch of turmeric

Serves 4-6

Instructions:

Combine spinach, tomatoes, artichoke hearts, avocado and walnuts in a large bowl.

Toss with olive oil, balsamic vinegar, salt and pepper.

Adjust oil, vinegar and seasoning to taste.

Mackinac Salad

This recipe is inspired by a salad I had many years ago on a visit to Mackinac Island. It is meant to have Feta, but it is (almost) as good if you eliminate the cheese and make it parve. Many kosher markets have a wide variety of dried fruit that is kosher for Pesach. The dried cherries are really the best feature of this salad, but if you cannot find them, substitute dried cranberries, apricots or raisins, or fresh pitted cherries.

Ingredients:

6-8 cups Baby Spinach,
    chopped
½ cup Walnuts, chopped
¼ - ½ cup Feta, crumbled (omit
    to make this parve)
$\frac{1}{3}$ cup Kalamata Olives,
    chopped
$\frac{1}{3}$ cup Dried Cherries, chopped
1 large Tomato, chopped
¼ cup Red Onion, finely
    chopped
1½ cups Terra Chips
1 tsp. Oregano
Ranch Dressing, to taste*

Instructions:

Combine all ingredients in a large bowl.

Mix well.

Adjust amount of dressing or any ingredients to taste.

*Make sure to use a parve ranch dressing if you are making this recipe parve. There are several good kosher l'Pesach options.

Serves 4-6

Greek Salad

This is one of my husband's favorite salads, so I make it all the time. The key to the salad is pepperoncini, so I was thrilled when I found a brand that makes a kosher l'Pesach option. During the year, it's easy to find several kosher brands, but during Pesach, there is an Israeli brand that sells them under the name "hot peppers." Feta is also a key to this salad, but it is possible to omit and make it parve. If you can find parve coconut milk yogurt...that is a good substitute to give a bit of the tang that you lose from eliminating the feta. As with any salad, use the amounts in the ingredient list as a guide rather than a hard and fast rule. If you want a bit less cucumber, or a little more kalamata...adjust to your taste.

Ingredients:

6-8 cups Romaine Lettuce, chopped
¼ - ½ cup Red Onion, finely chopped
2 cups Persian Cucumbers, chopped
2 cups Tomatoes, chopped
⅓ cup Kalamata Olives, chopped
⅓ cup Pepperoncinis, chopped
¼ - ½ cup Feta, cut into cubes
1 tsp. Oregano
1-2 Tbs. Balsamic Vinegar
2-3 Tbs. Olive Oil
Salt and Pepper to taste

Instructions:

In a large bowl, toss romaine lettuce with red onion, oregano, balsamic vinegar, olive oil, salt and pepper. Mix well. Adjust seasoning to taste.

I usually serve this salad plated individually, so I divide the lettuce base into each bowl at this point. To serve family style, just use one large bowl.

Arrange cucumbers, tomatoes, olives, pepperoncinis and feta cubes on top of the lettuce base.

Serves 4-6

Vegan Chopped Salad

This salad is substantial and it can easily be a full meal by itself. It can be served family style, but I usually plate it individually, because the color and number of the various ingredients allow you to create beautiful, unique designs.

Ingredients:

8 oz. Mixed Greens, chopped
6 oz. Romaine Lettuce, chopped
½ cup Quinoa, cooked
2 Tbs. Raw Almonds, chopped
2 tsp. Olive Oil
Salt and Pepper to taste
2 Avocados
8 oz. Cherry Tomatoes, halved or quartered
6 oz. Persian Cucumbers, chopped
6 oz. Canned Beets, chopped
4 oz. Asparagus, steamed or blanched and cut into ½" pieces
2 Portobello Mushrooms, roasted and chopped

For the dressing:
1 cup Avocado or Olive Oil
$\frac{1}{3}$ cup Balsamic Vinegar
2 cloves Garlic, minced
1 tsp. Salt
½ tsp. Pepper
1-1½ Tbs. Sugar
¼ tsp. Dried Oregano
¼ tsp. Dried Basil
$\frac{1}{8}$ tsp. Dried Thyme
$\frac{1}{8}$ tsp. Dried Sage

Instructions:

Begin by preparing the ingredients that need to be cooked. Roast the portobello mushrooms in a 425°F oven for 25-30 minutes, until they are soft. You can drizzle them with a little olive oil, salt and pepper and even a bit of balsamic to add flavor.

Steam or blanch the asparagus and cook the quinoa.

In a small bowl, combine the quinoa with the chopped almonds, 2 teaspoons of olive oil and salt and pepper. Mix well and adjust seasoning to taste. Set aside.

Combine the dressing ingredients in a bowl and whisk to combine. This can also be done by shaking the dressing in a jar or container with a lid.

Place the mixed greens and romaine in a large bowl. Add some dressing and toss to combine. The lettuce should be well dressed, but not drenched.

Divide the dressed lettuce mix into a salad bowl for each person, if plating individually, or into one large bowl, if serving family style.

Place a scoop of the quinoa mixture on top of the lettuce in the center of each bowl. Arrange the remaining salad ingredients around the quinoa, dividing them evenly between the bowls.

Drizzle a bit of dressing over the top of each bowl.

Serves 4-6

Grapefruit Avocado Salad

This is one of my absolute favorite salads and it is one that I make all year round. The bright sharpness of grapefruit contrasts perfectly with the creaminess of the avocado and the result is spectacular. It is also a fun salad to serve individually plated because the slices of grapefruit and avocado lend themselves to beautiful designs.

Ingredients:

8-10 cups Arugula, roughly chopped
1/3 cup Red Onion, finely chopped
½ cup Pistachios, roasted and chopped
1-2 Avocado, sliced
1 Grapefruit, cut into supremes

For the dressing:
¼ cup Olive Oil
2 Tbs. Apple Cider Vinegar
½ - 1 Tbs. Maple Syrup (start with ½ Tbs. and add more to taste)
1 Tbs. Grapefruit Juice (squeezed from the remainder of the grapefruit above)
1 clove Garlic, minced (optional)
Salt and Black Pepper to taste

Instructions:

To cut the grapefruit supremes, cut off the top and bottom of the grapefruit. Place the grapefruit on a cutting board with the flat bottom down. Using a sharp, thin knife, slice down from the top, along the edge to the bottom, cutting off the rind and pith (the whitish membrane under the rind) of the fruit. Continue around the entire grapefruit until all the rind and pith are removed. Gently cut into the fruit next to each inner membrane to remove the individual segments.

Set the segments aside.

Take the remaining inner portion of the grapefruit and squeeze it into a small bowl to collect fresh grapefruit juice for the dressing.

In a large bowl, combine arugula, red onion and pistachios.

In a small bowl or jar, combine dressing ingredients and mix well. (I like to use a jar with a tight cap that can be shaken to mix the ingredients.)

Adjust seasoning to taste. Add additional grapefruit juice or maple syrup, to taste.

Pour dressing over the arugula mixture and toss to combine.

Arrange avocado slices and grapefruit supremes on top of the salad, alternating in concentric circles. Or, portion salad onto individual salad plates and top with alternating avocado and grapefruit slices. (These may also be cut into chunks and tossed with the rest of the salad.)

Serves 4-6

Tex/Mex Kale Chicken Salad

This is a salad that can be a side or a main course. I like to add spiced cashews to make it a little more interesting, but it works with plain roasted/salted cashews as well. As with any kale salad, it's important to massage the kale first.

Ingredients:

8-10 cups Kale, chopped
2 cups Grilled Chicken Breast, chopped or shredded
3/4 cup Jicama, chopped or grated
1 Mango, diced
½ cup Spiced Cashews (or plain roasted/salted cashews), roughly chopped
¼ cup Red Onion, finely diced
1½ cups Terra Chips
Salt, to taste
1-2 Tbs. Olive Oil

For the Dressing:
1 large, ripe Avocado
1 Jalapeño, roasted, peeled and chopped
⅓ cup Parve Ranch Dressing
1 Tbs. White Wine Vinegar
2 Tbs. Lime Juice
zest of 1 Lime
¼ tsp. Black Pepper

For the Spiced Cashews:
1 cup Raw Cashews
1 Tbs. Oil
1 tsp. Garlic Powder
1 tsp. Paprika
¼ tsp. Cayenne Pepper
½ tsp. Onion Powder
¼ tsp. Salt
¼ tsp. Turmeric

Instructions:

To make the spiced cashews, I usually omit the oil and roast the nuts in a pan on the stove with some non-stick spray. As they heat, I add the spice mix and continue stirring as they roast. However, it is easiest to simply toss all of the ingredients together, spread the mixture on a parchment lined baking sheet and roast in a 350°F oven for 12-15 minutes, tossing halfway through cooking.

To make the dressing, begin by roasting a jalapeño. This can be done on the stove or in a 400°F oven. Make sure to poke holes in the pepper first so that it doesn't burst while roasting. Place the jalapeño in a zip-top plastic baggie or foil pouch to cool. This will make it easier to peel. Once the pepper has cooled, peel it and chop it. If you'd like a less spicy dressing, discard the seeds.

Place the flesh of the avocado, the peeled jalapeño, ranch dressing, vinegar, lime juice, zest and black pepper into the bowl of a food processor or blender. Puree until the mixture is smooth. Adjust lime juice and black pepper to taste. Set aside.

To make the salad, begin by massaging the kale. Place the chopped kale into a large bowl. Drizzle with olive oil and sprinkle with salt. "Massage" the kale by reaching into the bowl, grabbing handfuls of the kale, and squeezing your hands into fists. Continue massaging until it softens to your desired texture. It is fine for the kale to be a bit soft or "wilted".

Add chicken, terra chips, jicama, mango, cashews and red onions to the kale.

Add dressing and toss well to combine.

Serves 4-6

Kale Salad

Kale is one of those "super-foods" that is really healthy, so I try to incorporate into as many meals as I can. My go-to Kale salad calls for a mustard vinaigrette, so it's not an option for Pesach. I made a few changes and created a dressing that has a similar feel, and it plays off of the flavors in this salad brilliantly. I love adding feta, but if you are serving it with a meat meal, it will be just as good without the cheese. The most important thing to do when making kale salad is to "massage" the kale. It will be more pleasant to eat and easier to digest. Be aware that this does reduce the volume of the chopped kale, so you need to start with an amount that might seem like too much.

Ingredients:

2 bunches Kale (10-12 cups, chopped)
2 Tbs. Olive Oil
Salt to taste
1/3 cup Pine Nuts
1/4 - 1/2 cup Dried Cranberries
1/4 cup Feta Cheese (optional)

For the Dressing:
1 Shallot, minced
3 Tbs. White Wine Vinegar
1 Tbs. Tamarind Paste
1/2 Tbs. Horseradish Mayonnaise (Chrayonnaise) or Wasabi Mayo
1 Tbs. Honey

Instructions:

In a small bowl, combine the shallot and vinegar.

Set aside while preparing the remainder of the salad.

Place the chopped kale into a large bowl. Drizzle with olive oil and sprinkle with salt. "Massage" the kale by reaching into the bowl, grabbing handfuls of kale, and squeezing your hands into fists.

Continue massaging the kale until it softens to your desired texture. Even if it seems a bit "wilted" from the massage, it will be more pleasant to eat in the salad and it will still hold up to the dressing well. It can take up to 5-10 minutes to thoroughly massage the kale.

Add the pine nuts and cranberries (and Feta if you are making a dairy meal), and mix well.

Finish the dressing by adding the tamarind paste, chrayonnaise and honey to the vinegar/shallot mixture. Whisk to combine, and drizzle over the Kale.

Toss to combine.

Adjust salt and oil to taste.

Serves 4-6

Dairy Cobb Salad

I make Cobb salad often during the year. I started because I found a great kosher Bleu Cheese. I simply use parve fake meat substitutes for the chicken and bacon...and the result is delicious. I can't use these fake meat options during Pesach because they are chametz, but the Bleu cheese just happens to be kosher l'Pesach. So, I created this version of one of my favorite salads. It's a great option for a dairy lunch because it is so substantial.

Ingredients:

6-8 cups Romaine Lettuce, chopped
1 cup Cherry Tomatoes, halved or quartered
2 Roasted Portobello Mushrooms, chopped
3 Hard Boiled Eggs, sliced or chopped
1 large Avocado, cubed
¼ cup Scallions or Chives, minced
¼ cup Bleu Cheese, crumbled
8-10 strips Carrot Bacon (see page 151), chopped

For the Dressing:
½ cup Olive Oil
3 Tbs. Red Wine Vinegar
1 Tbs. Honey (or a bit less/more based on how sweet you want the dressing to be)
1 clove Garlic, minced
½ tsp. Oregano
Salt and Pepper to taste

Instructions:

Roast the portobello mushrooms in a 425°F oven for 25-30 minutes, covered, until they are soft. You can drizzle them with a little olive oil, salt and pepper and even a bit of balsamic to add some flavor.

Combine dressing ingredients in a bowl and whisk until thoroughly mixed.

Toss the lettuce with about 2/3 of the dressing.

Adjust salt and pepper to taste.

Place the dressed lettuce in a large serving bowl.

Arrange the remaining salad ingredients on top of the lettuce.

Drizzle with remaining dressing.

The ingredients may also be divided and plated individually.

Serves 4

Jicama Salad

Jicama is a healthy food to add to your diet, so I am always looking for new ways to incorporate it into recipes. I originally made this salad using a fine julienne cut for all of the vegetables and fruits, and it holds up a bit better...but it's A LOT of work! To make this a little easier, I now use a grater. The jicama and green apple do lose a bit of sturdiness, so if you want a salad that is not as likely to get soggy quickly...and you have time...small dice or a fine julienne work great for this dish.

Ingredients:

1 Jicama bulb: grated, finely julienned or diced
1 Bosc Pear: grated, finely julienned or diced
1 Granny Smith Apple: peeled and grated, finely julienned or diced
1 Yellow Bell Pepper: finely julienned or diced
1 Large Shallot, finely chopped
1 cup Cilantro, chopped

For the dressing:
½ cup Ripe Mango
2 Tbs. Olive Oil
2 Tbs. Lime Juice
1 Tbs. White Wine Vinegar
1 Tbs. Honey
1 clove Garlic, minced
Salt and Pepper to taste. (Start with ¼ tsp. each and add as needed)

Optional: a pinch of Cayenne Pepper

Instructions:

In a large bowl, mix the jicama, pear, apple, bell pepper, shallot and cilantro.

Combine all of the dressing ingredients in a blender or food processor and blend until smooth.

Add dressing to the salad and toss to combine. (You may not need to use all of the dressing.)

Adjust salt and pepper to taste.

If the mango was not very ripe, you may also want to add a bit more honey.

Serve immediately.

Serves 6

Broccoli Salad

This is a recipe I grew up with, and the original calls for bacon. When I make it during the year, I use a parve bacon substitute to give it the smoky, salty kick it needs. The salad is fine without it, but during Pesach, I use carrot bacon to approximate the flavor. You can always substitute Terra Chips if you want to skip this step.

Ingredients:

2 bunches of Broccoli Florets (about 6-7 cups)
1 cup Green Onions, finely chopped
¾ cup Golden Raisins
¾ cup Chopped Pecans

Optional: Carrot Bacon (see recipe on page 151) and/or Terra Chips

For the dressing:
1 cup Parve Mayonnaise
⅓ cup Sugar
3 Tbs. White Vinegar

Instructions:

Combine broccoli, green onions, raisins and pecans in a large bowl.

Mix well, cover and refrigerate for a few hours or overnight.

Mix mayonnaise and sugar in a small bowl until they are well combined. Add vinegar and mix until smooth. Cover and refrigerate for a few hours or overnight.

Add dressing to the salad to taste at least 30 minutes before serving. (You probably will not need to use all of the dressing.)

Add chopped carrot bacon and mix well.

Cover and chill until serving.

If using Terra Chips, add them just before serving so they don't get soggy.

Serves 4-6

Fish

Mango Salmon

This is my favorite salmon recipe. It can be made with salmon steaks or fillets. If you opt for fillets, decrease the cooking time accordingly. It is a versatile dish that works as a beautiful appetizer or fish course, or over leafy greens as a main course. You can serve it either hot or cold, so it's a good option that can be made ahead of time for Shabbos or Yom Tov. The recipe I use during the year has coriander, so I have substituted sumac for Pesach. If you can't find sumac, it is almost as good if you use allspice or simply omit it altogether.

Ingredients:

For the Marinade:
6 Tbs. Fresh Lime Juice
2 Tbs. Fresh Ginger, minced or
   grated
4 cloves Garlic, minced
1 Poblano Chili, diced
2 Jalapeño Peppers, diced,
   (seeds and stems removed)

4 Salmon Steaks (pin bones
   removed)
2 Tbs. Oil
1 Onion, diced
1 Mango, peeled and diced
1 tsp. Turmeric
1 tsp. Sumac
3 Tbs. Red Wine Vinegar
1/3 cup Cilantro, chopped
2-3 tsp. Sugar (depending on the
   sweetness of the mango)
Salt to taste

Instructions:

Combine marinade ingredients in a bowl.

Place salmon in a bowl or baking dish.

Spoon the marinade over the fish, coating all sides. Pour in the remainder of the marinade. Cover and refrigerate for 3-4 hours.

In a large sauté pan, heat the oil over a medium high heat. Add onion and mango and cook until the onion is translucent.

Add turmeric and sumac. Mix well and cook for an additional 2-3 minutes.

Add the salmon and the marinade into the pan. If using salmon steaks, cook on each side for about 5 minutes, depending on thickness. (When I use thinner salmon fillets, I only cook on one side.)

Add vinegar, cilantro, sugar and salt. Bring to a simmer. Cook for about 10 minutes.

Serve warm, or chill in the refrigerator for up to 24 hours and serve over mixed greens.

Serves 4-8 (depending on whether it is cut into appetizer portions or entrees)

Moqueca

Moqueca is a traditional Brazilian fish stew that is really flavorful. It is hearty and healthy, and it can be the starter or soup course, or even a main course for lunch with a nice salad.

Ingredients:

2 lbs. Cod Fillets, cut into 2" pieces and patted dry
6 cloves Garlic, minced
4 Tbs. Lime Juice, plus the zest of
   1 Lime
Salt and Black Pepper to taste
2 Tbs. Olive Oil or Coconut Oil
1 Yellow Onion, chopped
1 Poblano Pepper, seeds and stem removed and finely diced
1 Red Bell Pepper, seeds and stem removed and finely diced
3 Green Onions, chopped
2 large Tomatoes, chopped (about 2 cups)
1 Tbs. Tomato Paste
½ cup Vegetable Stock
2 tsp. Paprika
1 pinch Cayenne
1 cup Cilantro, chopped
14 oz. can Coconut Milk

Optional: 1 Fresno Pepper

Instructions:

In a bowl, combine 1 clove minced garlic, 2 tablespoons of lime juice, the lime zest and roughly ¼ teaspoon of salt. Add the fish and toss to coat the pieces. Set aside.

Heat olive oil in a pot on the stove over medium heat. Sauté the onion for 10-12 minutes.

Add the remaining 5 cloves of garlic and sauté for 3-5 minutes.

Add the poblano pepper, bell pepper, green onion, paprika and a dash of salt and pepper. Cook until the peppers soften.

Add tomatoes, tomato paste and 2 tablespoons of lime juice to the pot and cook for 5-8 minutes.

Add cilantro and fish to the pot, gently layering them among the vegetables.

Add coconut milk and vegetable stock to the pot.

For a spicier stew, pierce a fresno pepper and add it to the pot.

Bring to a boil, then reduce heat to a simmer.

Cook for 15-20 minutes.

Adjust seasoning to taste and add a pinch of cayenne if you'd like an extra kick.

Serves 6-8

Pomegranate Pepper Red Snapper

This is one of those dishes that can simply be a fish course, or it can be the star of a nice lunch or the base of a quinoa bowl. If you don't have Red Snapper, any white fish will be a good substitute for this flavorful dish.

Ingredients:

1½ lbs. Red Snapper, fillets or a
   whole cleaned and scaled fish
Salt and Pepper to taste
zest of 1 Lime
1 Tbs. Olive Oil

For the Sauce:
2 Tbs. Olive Oil
6 Shallots, sliced
1 large Carrot, peeled and
   grated
1 Red Bell Pepper, thinly sliced
1 Poblano Pepper, thinly sliced
1 Jalapeño, finely diced
½ tsp. Ground Thyme
1 tsp. Ground Allspice
2 tsp. Brown Sugar
¼ cup Apple Cider Vinegar
½ cup Pomegranate Juice
¼ cup Red Wine Vinegar
Salt and Pepper to taste

Optional: ¼ cup Green Olives,
   chopped

Instructions:

Heat 2 tablespoons of olive oil in a pan over medium high heat.

Add shallots, carrot, bell pepper, poblano pepper, and jalapeño. Cook for 3-5 minutes.

Add thyme and allspice and cook for another 8-10 minutes until the vegetables are soft.

Add brown sugar, apple cider vinegar, pomegranate juice and red wine vinegar. Bring to a boil, then reduce to a simmer. Simmer until the sauce thickens a bit. Season with salt and pepper to taste. Set aside, keeping warm.

Heat 1 tablespoon of olive oil in a skillet over medium high heat. Sprinkle fish with salt, pepper and lime zest, and place in the skillet. Cook the fish for roughly 2-3 minutes per side for fillets or 5-7 minutes on each side for a whole fish.

Remove fish from heat and place on serving platter.

Pour sauce over fish.

Serve immediately.

Serves 6-8

Trout Stew

This is another traditional Finnish recipe. The potatoes make the stew hearty, so with a side salad, it can be a complete meal. It is one of my favorite dishes because it is simple to prepare and absolutely delicious.

Ingredients:

1 pound Trout, cut into 2" pieces
1-2 Tbs. Olive Oil
1 Onion, chopped
4 cups Water
4 Golden Potatoes, diced
2 cups Coconut Milk
1 tsp. Dill (dried)
1 tsp. Salt (plus more, to taste)
½ tsp. Black Pepper
1 pinch of Cayenne
½ cup Chives or Green Onions, finely chopped

Instructions:

Heat oil in a pot over medium high heat. Sauté onion until it caramelizes a bit. Add fish, salt, pepper, dill and water. Bring to a simmer and cook until the fish just flakes.

Remove fish with a slotted spoon. Set aside. Add potatoes to the pot and cook until tender.

Return fish to the pot and add coconut milk. Simmer for 15-20 minutes.

Adjust seasoning. It will likely need more salt. Add cayenne pepper to taste.

Sprinkle green onions on top of each bowl just before serving.

Serves 4-6

Pecan Crusted Salmon

PARVE

This dish reminds me of autumn because I started making it when I was experimenting with different spice blends to use in a traditional Finnish mulled wine that is best enjoyed during cold weather. However, I love the combination of pecans and salmon, so there's no reason not to enjoy it over Pesach since it just happens to be chametz and kitniyot free.

Ingredients:

1 lb. Salmon, divided into 4 oz. fillets
½ cup Chopped Pecans
1 Tbs. Maple Syrup
½ tsp. Ground Ginger
¼ tsp. Salt
¼ tsp. Black Pepper
1-2 Tbs. Olive Oil

Serves 4

Instructions:

In a non-stick pan over medium heat, roast the pecans with the maple syrup, stirring frequently. If you are not using a non-stick pan, use a bit of non-stick spray. Once the nuts are well roasted, but not burned, remove from heat and add the ginger, salt and pepper.

Spread the nut mixture onto a plate or shallow baking dish.

Brush each fillet with a bit of olive oil, and press the oiled side onto the spice mixture. Gently press to get as much of the mixture as possible to adhere to the salmon. Sprinkle additional nuts onto the fillets to reach desired amount of coating.

The fish can be cooked in an oven or on the stove. In the oven, cook the salmon for about 15 minutes at 400°F. On the stove, heat olive oil over medium heat. Carefully cook with the crust side down for about 5 minutes. Make sure that it does not burn. Gently flip the salmon fillets and cook on the other side for another 5-8 minutes until cooked through.

Tahitian Tuna

This is a recipe I learned when I visited Tahiti. The vanilla there is truly exceptional, and so trying to make this with grocery store ingredients in America feels like a pale version of what it should be, but it's still delicious.

Ingredients:

4 Tuna Steaks
1-2 Tbs. Oil, as needed
2 cups Coconut Cream
1 Vanilla Bean, split open
   lengthwise
1 tsp. Paprika
Salt and Pepper to taste
1 Green Onion, sliced

Instructions:

Rub olive oil on the tuna steaks and sprinkle with salt and pepper.

Heat a skillet over medium high heat. Once the pan is hot, add the tuna.

Depending on the heat of the pan and your preference, the tuna should cook for between 2-5 minutes per side. Perfectly cooked tuna steaks should be seared on the outside and rare on the inside. If this is how you prefer your tuna, cook it in a very hot pan for approximately 2 minutes per side. Once the tuna is cooked to your taste, set aside and keep warm.

In the same pan where the tuna was cooked, heat the coconut cream with the vanilla pod.

Add paprika, salt and pepper to taste.

Stir gently and cook for 3-5 minutes. Once the sauce is thick enough and heated through, pour over tuna.

Garnish with green onions.

Serves 4

Tamarind-Ginger Marinated Salmon

PARVE

I love fresh ginger, so I incorporate it into everything I can. I especially like the tang of ginger contrasted with a fatty fish like salmon. This recipe calls for a shiitake dashi, but you can substitute an imitation kosher l'Pesach soy sauce if you don't have dried shiitakes. The salmon can be baked or cooked on the stove.

Ingredients:

For the marinade:
¼ cup Tamarind Paste
2 Tbs. Apple Cider Vinegar
2 Tbs. Balsamic Vinegar
2 Tbs. Shiitake Dashi* or Kosher
   l'Pesach Imitation Soy Sauce
2 Green Onions, finely chopped
4 Tbs. Fresh Ginger, minced
1 clove Garlic, minced
1 Tbs. Olive Oil
1 Tbs. Maple Syrup

4 Salmon Fillets
Salt and Black Pepper to taste

Instructions:

Put all marinade ingredients in a bowl and whisk to combine.

Place the salmon fillets in a baking dish and pour the marinade over them. Turn to coat.

Cover and refrigerate for 60 minutes.

If baking, preheat oven to 325°F. You may also cook the fillets on the stove.

Remove fish from marinade and season with salt and pepper.

Place the fish on a parchment lined baking sheet and bake for approximately 20-25 minutes, or until the salmon is flaky.

*To make the shiitake dashi, place 6 dried shiitake mushrooms in ½ cup hot water. Soak for a minimum of 20 minutes. I usually soak them for about an hour. You will need about 2 tablespoons for this recipe. You may substitute kosher l'Pesach imitation soy sauce if you do not have dried shiitakes.

Serves 4

Entrees

Gnocchi

This gnocchi has become the foundation of Pesach menu planning for me. I serve it almost every day over Yom Tov. It is delicious and incredibly versatile. Its pasta-like texture really satisfies the need to bite into something chewy and substantial. The beauty of this dish is that it can fill out or anchor either a dairy or fleishig meal. It works just as well with a creamy mushroom or alfredo sauce as it does with a hearty meat ragout, spicy tomato sauce or pesto. It is also a terrific base for parve alfredo sauce (see recipe on page 145) with grilled chicken breast. I usually make a big batch and leave the dough in the fridge to roll out and cook whenever I need a great, quick meal. Many gnocchi recipes recommend boiling the potatoes first, but the reason why this recipe works so well is that the potatoes are baked. This reduces their moisture content and results in a much better texture. I recommend using Russet potatoes in this recipe because they result in a better texture that is easier to work with. However, if you can handle softer dough, Yukon Gold potatoes do give the dish better flavor.

Ingredients:

1½ lbs. Russet Potatoes (about
    1 lb. after cooking/peeling, a
    little over 2¼ cups)
¼ cup Potato Starch
2 Tbs. Tapioca Flour, plus more for
    rolling out the dough
1 Egg, room temperature, lightly
    beaten
½ tsp. Salt

Optional: 1 Tbs. Olive Oil for
    sautéing

Instructions:

Preheat oven to 400°F.

Clean potatoes and poke holes into each with a fork or paring knife. Do NOT peel them prior to baking. Place them on a baking sheet and cook them in the oven for about 60-90 minutes, until they are soft and easily pierced with a knife.

Once the potatoes have cooled a bit, peel them with a paring knife and place the flesh in a large bowl. Mash the potatoes until they are smooth. Make sure that there are no large lumps. The easiest way to do this is to use a food mill or potato ricer, but I have managed with just 2 forks.

Serves 4

Add the egg to the mashed potatoes and mix well.

In a small bowl, combine potato flour, tapioca flour and salt. Add this to the mashed potatoes and mix thoroughly.

Dust a work surface with tapioca flour. Working in batches, and adding more tapioca flour as needed, roll the dough into ½"- ¾" thick strands. Cut into 1" pieces and set the pieces aside to rest while you finish shaping the remainder of the dough.

Bring a large pot of salted water to a boil on the stove. Add the gnocchi to the boiling water. Work in batches, as they will not all fit in the pot at once. Do not stir. Simply allow them to cook for about 3-5 minutes. They will float to the top on their own. Remove from the water with a slotted spoon.

You may serve the gnocchi immediately with any number of sauces. (Find options in the Sauces and Staples section of this book.) You may also sauté them in a bit of olive oil over a medium heat before serving. I like to add this step to give the gnocchi a bit of crispiness.

Chicken Paprikash

I have spent years modifying old family recipes to fit into the guidelines of kashrut. This is one that I always loved, but it was tricky to make it work, especially for Pesach. When I discovered how well cashew cream works with this dish, it was a game changer. It does take a bit of time to make the cream to use in this dish, but it really is worth the effort.

Ingredients:

3 lbs. Chicken, cut into pieces
2 Tbs. Margarine or Cooking Oil
2 large Yellow Onions, diced
8 oz. Fresh Mushrooms, sliced
4 cloves Garlic, minced
1 Red Bell Pepper, diced
1½ cups Chicken Broth
½ cup Cooking Sherry
3 Tbs. Paprika
½ tsp. Salt (plus more to taste)
½ tsp. Black Pepper
1 Tbs. Tapioca Flour
1 cup Cashew Cream (see
 recipe on page 153)

Instructions:

If you don't already have the cashew cream prepared, begin by soaking cashews at least 3 hours before you start preparing this recipe.

Heat the margarine or oil in a sturdy pan over medium high heat. Brown the chicken pieces and set aside.

Add the onions to the hot oil and sauté until they start to caramelize.

Add mushrooms, bell pepper and garlic and cook for another 6-8 minutes until they soften. Add paprika, salt and pepper. Mix well.

Add the chicken pieces back into the pan.

Stir in chicken broth and sherry. Bring the mixture to a boil, then cover and reduce heat to simmer for 40-45 minutes. During this time, finish making the cashew cream if it was not prepared earlier.

Remove the chicken from the pan and set aside.

Add the tapioca flour to the cashew cream and mix thoroughly.

Add this mixture to the sauce in the pan and cook to thicken. Once sauce reaches desired thickness, adjust seasoning to taste and return the chicken to the pan. Heat through and serve over mashed potatoes, quinoa, cauliflower rice or pesach noodles.

*Chicken should always be cooked to an internal temperature of at least 165°F. Use a meat thermometer to ensure food safety.

Serves 6-8

Chicken Piccata

This dish is remarkably flavorful. Lemons and capers give it a delightful tanginess. The sauce also works well with a delicate white fish or salmon, so you can use this recipe to make a fish option if you have guests who do not eat meat.

Ingredients:

4 Chicken Breasts, pounded to
    ½" thickness
½ cup Tapioca Flour
zest of 1 Lemon
½ tsp Salt
½ tsp Black Pepper
1-2 Tbs. Olive Oil

For the Sauce:
1-2 Tbs. Olive Oil
1 large Shallot, thinly sliced
2 cloves Garlic, minced
¼ cup Margarine
1 Tbs. Tapioca Flour
1 cup Chicken Broth
1½ -2 Tbs. Lemon Juice
½ cup White Wine
3-4 Tbs. Capers, drained
    (substitute green olives if you
    cannot access capers that are
    certified for Pesach use.)
¼ cup Fresh Parsley, chopped

Instructions:

Combine ½ cup tapioca flour, lemon zest, salt and pepper in a shallow bowl. Coat the chicken on each side with this mixture.

Heat 1-2 Tbs. olive oil in a sauté pan over medium high heat. Cook the chicken breasts for approximately 4-5 minutes on each side. Remove the chicken from the pan, set aside and keep warm.

Add 1-2 Tbs. olive oil to the pan in which the chicken was cooked. Sauté the shallot for 2-3 minutes.

Add garlic and cook for another 2 minutes.

Add the margarine to the pan. Once it has melted, whisk in 1 Tbs. tapioca flour. Continue stirring until there are no lumps.

Slowly add the chicken broth, lemon juice and wine, whisking continuously.

Simmer for 3-5 minutes, then add capers and parsley. If the sauce is too thick, add a bit more broth until it reaches desired consistency. If it is too thin, cook longer to thicken.

Season to taste with salt and pepper.

Return the chicken to the pan and heat through.

Serve over mashed potatoes, zoodles, quinoa or pesach pasta.

*Chicken should always be cooked to an internal temperature of at least 165°F. Use a meat thermometer to ensure food safety.

Serves 4

Chicken Cacciatore

This is my mother's recipe, and she always made it with boneless, skinless chicken breast because that was the only way my brother and I would eat it. I have come to learn that most cacciatore recipes use bone-in chicken, but I've left this recipe intentionally ambiguous. Use whatever type of chicken is preferred in your household.

Ingredients:

3½ - 4 lbs. Chicken, cut into pieces
2 Tbs. Olive Oil
2 Tbs. Margarine
1 Yellow Onion, diced
1 Green Bell Pepper, diced
1 cup Celery, diced
6 oz. Mushrooms, sliced
4 cloves Garlic, minced
15 oz. can Tomato Sauce
¾ cup Red Wine
¼ tsp. Salt
½ tsp. Black Pepper
1 tsp. Dried Oregano
1 tsp. Dried Basil
14 oz. can Chopped Tomatoes
2 Tbs. Parsley, chopped

Instructions:

Heat the oil and margarine over a medium high heat in a large pan on the stove.

Add the chicken and brown for about 3-4 minutes per side. Remove the chicken, set aside and keep warm.

To the hot pan, add the onion, bell pepper and celery and cook until the onions are a bit caramelized and the peppers and celery soften.

Add the mushrooms and garlic and cook for another 3-5 minutes.

Add tomato sauce, wine and spices. Mix well, and cook for about 10 minutes while the sauce reduces and thickens a bit.

Add canned tomatoes and parsley and heat through.

Return the chicken to the pan, cover and cook for about 40 minutes over medium heat. (remove the lid if you want a thicker sauce.)

Adjust seasoning to taste.

Serve over mashed potatoes, cauliflower rice, quinoa or pesach pasta

*Chicken should always be cooked to an internal temperature of at least 165°F. Use a meat thermometer to ensure food safety.

Serves 6-8

Chicken Yassa

Chicken is at the heart of so many yom tov meals, but it can get boring. I know many people who make the same chicken dishes over and over, so I am always on the lookout for new ways to prepare it. When I learned about this traditional Senegalese dish, I was intrigued. The dish is based on a rich dijon onion sauce, so I had to find a way to eliminate the kitniyot, while preserving as much flavor as possible.

Ingredients:

2 lbs. Chicken, cut into pieces
2 Tbs. Olive Oil
3 Yellow Onions, sliced
6 cloves Garlic, minced
4-5 Lemon Slices, seeds
    removed
2-3 tsp. Prepared Horseradish
2 cups Chicken Broth
2 Jalapenos, whole, pierced
1 tsp. Turmeric
Salt and Pepper to taste
Cayenne pepper to taste

For the Marinade:
1 cup Lemon Juice
¼ cup Lime Juice
½ Yellow Onion, roughly
    chopped
4 cloves Garlic, minced
1 Tbs. Olive Oil
2 Jalapeno Peppers, roughly
    chopped
½ tsp. Turmeric

Instructions:

Combine marinade ingredients in large bowl.

Place the chicken pieces in the bowl, cover and refrigerate overnight. (Or at least 4 hours)

Remove the chicken from the marinade. Pat the chicken dry and remove any lingering bits of the marinade mixture.

Heat 2 Tbs. olive oil in a large, sturdy pot. Brown the pieces of chicken on each side. Remove from the pot and set aside.

In the same pot, cook the onions until they turn a rich dark color. This will take approximately 30-45 minutes, but the darker the onions get without burning, the better the flavor of the dish will be. Stir frequently once they begin to brown and do not allow them to burn.

Add garlic, horseradish and lemon slices. Cook for 2-3 minutes.

Return the chicken to the pot, layering the chicken pieces with the onions.

Add broth and jalapenos, and season with salt and pepper.

Bring to a boil, then reduce heat to medium-low. Cook for 60-70 minutes, stirring occasionally.

Adjust seasoning to taste. Add cayenne if desired.

Serve hot over mashed potatoes, cauliflower rice, quinoa or pesach noodles.

*Chicken should always be cooked to an internal temperature of at least 165°F. Use a meat thermometer to ensure food safety.

Serves 6

Sheet Pan Barbeque Tamarind Chicken

Sheet pan recipes allow you to make a whole meal in a short time. This is an intentionally simple recipe. Any vegetables that stand up well to roasting may be used in this dish.

Ingredients:

2 lbs. Boneless Chicken pieces
1 lb. Fresh Asparagus, cut into 2" pieces
1 Orange Bell Pepper, cut into chunks
1 Yellow Bell Pepper, cut into chunks
½ Red Onion, cut in half and sliced
2 Zucchini, cut into halves and sliced
12 oz. Fresh Mushrooms, cut into chunks or slices
1-2 Tbs. Olive Oil
½ tsp. Salt
½ tsp. Black Pepper
½ tsp. Paprika
½ tsp. Turmeric

For the Sauce:
1 cup Barbeque Sauce
3 Tbs. Tamarind Paste
Optional: 1-2 Tbs. Honey, to taste

Instructions:

Preheat oven to 425°F.

Toss the vegetables in the olive oil and spices to coat. Spread this mixture onto a sheet pan.

Combine sauce ingredients in a bowl. Remove half the sauce and set aside to use as a baste later.

Toss the chicken pieces in the remaining sauce and arrange on top of the vegetables on the sheet pan.

Cook for 15 minutes.

Remove from oven and toss the chicken and vegetables. Baste with the reserved sauce and return to oven for another 10-15 minutes, until the chicken is fully cooked.

Serve hot.

*Chicken should always be cooked to an internal temperature of at least 165°F. Use a meat thermometer to ensure food safety.

Serves 4-6

Cashew Chicken

This is a low carb, light and healthy main course that is quick and easy to prepare. Every year I buy kosher l'Pesach imitation soy sauce, and I never find enough uses for it. I've noticed it lingering months later in the pantries of many friends, as well, so I have included several recipes that feature it.

Ingredients:

1 lb. Boneless, Skinless Chicken, cut into pieces
½ lb. White Mushrooms, sliced
½ lb. Bok Choy, chopped
1 cup Green Onions, sliced
3 cloves Garlic, minced
2 Tbs. Vegetable Oil
½ cup Cashews
Salt to taste
pinch of Cayenne Pepper

For the Sauce:
½ cup Water
2 Tbs. Kosher l'Pesach Imitation Soy Sauce
3 tsp. Tapioca Flour
1 Bouillon Cube

Instructions:

Combine sauce ingredients in a small bowl and set aside.

Heat oil in a large pan. Brown the chicken over medium high heat until cooked through.

Add the mushrooms and sauté until they soften.

Add bok choy, green onions and garlic and cook another 5-8 minutes.

Add the sauce to the pan and cook until the dish thickens to the desired consistency.

Add cashews and heat through.

Add salt and cayenne pepper to taste.

Serve over quinoa or cauliflower rice.

*Chicken should always be cooked to an internal temperature of at least 165°F. Use a meat thermometer to ensure food safety.

Serves 4

Stewed Lamb with Horseradish Sauce

The first time I made this dish with kosher lamb, it was far too salty. Since kosher meat may be a bit saltier, start with a little less salt and add more at the end if it needs it. This recipe reflects much less salt than I originally started with.

Ingredients:

2 ½ lbs. Lamb, cut into cubes
2 Tbs. Olive Oil
2 cups Water
½-1 tsp. Salt (plus more to taste)
1 tsp. Black Pepper
2 tsp. Dried Dill

For the Sauce:
1 Tbs. Margarine
1 Tbs. Tapioca Flour
1-1 ½ Tbs. Prepared Horseradish
Broth from Lamb
Salt to taste

Instructions:

Heat olive oil in a sauté pan and brown the lamb cubes.

Add water, salt, pepper and dill. Cover and cook until the lamb is tender. (About 45-50 minutes.)

Remove lamb from pan and keep warm. Reserve the broth to make the sauce.

In a small saucepan, melt margarine over medium heat.

Gradually add tapioca flour, whisking constantly to avoid lumps.

Slowly add in 2 cups of the lamb broth, continuing to whisk.

Add water if necessary to reach a volume of approximately 2 cups.

Heat to thicken to desired consistency.

Add horseradish, mix well.

Add salt to taste.

Pour sauce over the lamb and serve immediately.

Serves 6

Moussaka

I write a lot about how much I love eggplant, so it is should come as no surprise that I'm a huge fan of Moussaka. It is essentially a complete meal in one dish...the meat, starch and vegetable are all included...and it is delicious. During the year, I can easily make a parve bechamel type sauce to use on top of the casserole. But, my favorite dairy substitutes for this are kitniyot, so it gets trickier over Pesach. I tried to think completely outside the box for this recipe. After trying multiple versions, I landed on a roasted cauliflower puree that is unexpected, but captures the feeling of a traditional moussaka.

Ingredients:

3-4 large Eggplants
4 large Potatoes, peeled and cut
   into ¼" slices
3 Tbs. Olive Oil, divided, plus
   more for frying eggplant
1 lb. Ground Lamb or Beef (or a
   mixture of both)
2 Onions, finely chopped
7 cloves minced Garlic, divided
1 (15oz.) can Crushed Tomatoes
2 Tbs. Tomato Paste
½ tsp. Cinnamon
¼ tsp. Allspice
2 Tbs. Fresh Flat Leaf Parsley,
   minced
1 tsp. Oregano
1 tsp. Salt, divided, plus more to
   taste
½ tsp. Black Pepper
½ cup Red Wine
1 Egg, beaten
2 Egg Yolks
6 cups Cauliflower Florets,
   chopped
1½ cup Coconut Milk
½ tsp. Nutmeg

Non-stick Cooking Spray

Instructions:

Begin by roasting the cauliflower for the topping. Toss cauliflower with 1-2 tablespoons of olive oil and a dash of salt. Roast on a parchment lined baking sheet in a 425°F oven for 20-25 minutes, until they are a bit browned. Set aside until you are ready to finish the topping.

To prepare the eggplant, cut off the top and bottom of each and use a vegetable peeler to peel strips down each side, about 1 inch apart. Some people prefer to peel their eggplant entirely, but I find that the dish becomes too mushy without a bit of the skin to give it some structure. Cut each eggplant into ¼" slices.

If you'd like to draw out some of the moisture, at this stage, lay out the eggplant slices on cutting boards lined with paper towels. Sprinkle a bit of salt onto each slice and allow to sit for about 30 minutes. I usually measure about 1 teaspoon of salt into a bowl and use that to limit the total amount that can be sprinkled onto the eggplant. Once the moisture beads, use a paper towel to pat the slices dry. I only do this on one side of each slice. When I have tried salting both sides, the result has just been too salty.

Heat olive oil in a pan over medium high heat. Fry the eggplant slices in batches until they are soft and a bit browned. Remove to a paper towel lined tray to drain while you finish frying the remainder of the eggplant. Set aside until you are ready to assemble the dish.

To prepare the potatoes, bring a large pot of water to a boil on the stove. Add the peeled slices and boil for about 5 minutes. Remove from heat and drain. Set aside until you are ready to assemble the dish.

To prepare the meat base, heat 1 tablespoon of olive oil in a large sauté pan. Brown the lamb and/or beef. Drain any excess fat from the pan, and set the meat aside.

Add another 1-2 Tbs. of olive oil to the pan, and add the onions. Cook for about 10-12 minutes until they caramelize a bit. Add 4 cloves of minced garlic and cook for another 3-4 minutes.

cont.

Return the meat to the pan and add the crushed tomatoes, tomato paste, cinnamon, allspice, parsley, oregano, pepper and wine. Mix to combine thoroughly.

Bring to a boil, then reduce heat to a simmer. Cover and cook for about 30 minutes.

Remove the lid and continue to simmer for another 10-15 minutes until the liquid is absorbed. Taste the sauce and add salt to taste. Since kosher meat tends to be a bit salty, you may not need to add much if any. Remove from heat and allow to cool a bit.

Mix in the beaten egg once the sauce has cooled to the point that it will not cook the egg.

To finish the cauliflower topping, in a saucepan on the stove, sauté 3 cloves of minced garlic in about 1 tablespoon of olive oil.

Add the coconut milk to the garlic and heat through.

Add the roasted cauliflower and bring to a boil. Cook for about 10 minutes.

Remove from heat and use an immersion blender or food processor to puree the coconut milk/cauliflower mixture. Blend until completely smooth.

Add about ½ teaspoon of salt and a light ½ teaspoon of nutmeg. Adjust seasoning to taste.

Once the mixture has cooled a bit, whisk in the 2 egg yolks.

Preheat oven to 350°F and assemble the moussaka.

Grease a 9x11 baking dish with non-stick cooking spray. I have not included matzah meal in this recipe because it has gluten and may bring up issues of gebrochts, but if you eat it, and you'd like to sprinkle some in the bottom of the dish to absorb some of the moisture, that is an option. You may also sprinkle a layer of potato starch in the bottom of the dish if you'd like to absorb some of the liquid, but it is not absolutely necessary.

Create a layer of potato slices that overlap a bit on the bottom of the baking dish.

Use about half of the eggplant to create an overlapping layer of slices on top of this.

Spread the meat sauce on top of the eggplant in an even layer.

Layer the remainder of the eggplant on top of the meat.

Finally, spread the cauliflower sauce evenly over the top.

Bake, uncovered, for about 50-60 minutes. Allow to cool a bit before cutting into the dish.

Serves 8-12

Beef Ragout

My family is from Karelia, which is the eastern part of Finland. Allspice is a staple in this cuisine, so these old family recipes are perfect for Pesach. In this dish, the allspice blends beautifully with the beef. If you really like the flavor and you want it to be more prominent, use a bit extra. It's a really easy dish that takes almost no time to prepare, and just cooks all day in a low oven.

Ingredients:

2 lbs. Beef Chuck, cubed
4 medium Onions, sliced
1-1½ tsp. Salt
1 tsp. Black Pepper
2-3 tsp. Ground Allspice
4 cups Beef Broth

Serves 6-8

Instructions:

Preheat oven to 275°F.

Combine salt, pepper and allspice in a small bowl.

Arrange the meat and onions in layers in a heavy casserole dish with a tight fitting lid. Sprinkle each layer with the spice mixture.

In a separate pot, bring the beef broth to a boil, then gently pour it over the meat mixture.

Cover and cook for 5 ½ to 6 hours until the meat is very tender.

Adjust seasoning to taste. Serve alone or over mashed potatoes or gnocchi.

Hamburger Stroganoff

This is a dish that a lot of people forget about at Pesach. The two ways I make it during the year…either meat with parve sour cream substitute, or dairy with fake meat substitute… are not options during Passover. But, with a little bit of creativity, I realized that I can make it work for Pesach. There are two recipes in this book for parve sour cream, and for this stroganoff, the Cashew based recipe is the best option.

Ingredients:

2-3 Tbs. Olive Oil
1 pound Ground Beef
1 medium Yellow Onion,
 chopped
4 cloves Garlic, minced
12 oz. Mushrooms, sliced (either
 white or a mixture of cremini
 and white)
¼ cup Cooking Sherry
1 cup Parve Pesach Sour
 Cream: Cashew Based (see
 page 153)*
1-2 tsp. Tapioca Flour (optional)

Salt and Black Pepper to taste

Italian Flat Leaf Parsley to
garnish

Instructions:

Heat 1 Tbs. olive oil in a large sauté pan over medium heat.

Brown the ground beef. Drain any excess fat from the pan, and set the meat aside.

Add another 1-2 Tbs. of olive oil to the pan, and add the onions. Cook for about 10-12 minutes until they caramelize.

Add mushrooms and ¼ tsp. each of salt and black pepper. Cook for about 8-10 minutes.

Add garlic and cook for another 2-3 minutes.

Return the cooked ground beef to the pan. Add cashew sour cream and cooking sherry. Mix well and heat through.

Adjust salt and pepper to taste. It will probably need at least another ¼ tsp of pepper, and possibly a pinch of salt.

If the consistency is too thin, add tapioca flour to thicken, mix thoroughly and heat through.

Garnish with chopped parsley and serve over mashed potatoes, zoodles or Pesach pasta or gnocchi.

*Note: For this recipe, I use almost ½ cup water when making the cashew sour cream because it thickens when cooked into the stroganoff.

Serves 4-6

Vegetable Lasagna

I am not someone who shies away from complicated recipes. When it comes to steps, I embrace a "the more, the merrier" mindset…if it makes a dish better. But even I can admit that this recipe is pretty patshke. But it is SO worth it! It is a really delicious lasagna that doesn't feel diminished by the absence of noodles at all. To make it a bit easier, you may use a store bought jar of marinara sauce. There are some good kosher l'Pesach options that are widely accessible, but if you have a favorite family recipe…by all means, patshke it up! The best tip I have for this recipe is to invest in an extra deep 13x9 baking dish. I added these to both my Pesach and Year-Round baking dish collections, and it makes a huge difference anytime I make a layered casserole or baked pasta dish.

Ingredients:

3-5 cups Marinara Sauce (from a jar, your own recipe, or see page 144 in this book)
4-6 cups Mozzarella Cheese, grated
½ cup Parmesan Cheese, grated (in addition to the amount listed in the filling below)

For the "Ricotta-Style" Layer:
1 lb. Cottage Cheese (or Ricotta)
1/3 cup Parmesan Cheese, grated
1 Egg, lightly beaten
2 cloves Garlic, minced
½ c. Italian Flat Leaf Parsley, chopped
3 Tbs. Fresh Basil, chopped
½ tsp. Salt
½ tsp. Black Pepper

For the Roasted Vegetable Layer:
1 Red Bell Pepper, cut into ½" chunks
2 small Zucchinis, sliced and cut in halves
1 Yellow Zucchini, sliced and cut into halves
16 oz. Fresh Mushrooms, sliced
½ Yellow Onion, finely diced
5 cloves Garlic, minced
2-3 Tbs. Olive Oil
Salt and Black Pepper, to taste

For the Pesach "Noodle" Layer:
6 Eggs
9 Tbs. Water
1½ cup Tapioca Flour

Non-Stick Cooking Spray

Instructions:

Preheat oven to 400°F. Line a baking sheet with tin foil and parchment paper.

In a large bowl, toss all the vegetables (for the roasted veggie layer) with olive oil, garlic, salt and pepper.

Arrange this mixture in an even layer on the baking sheet and bake for 40-45 minutes. Allow vegetables to drain in a colander after they are roasted (or just remove them with a slotted spoon). This will minimize the liquid released from the roasting, as it makes the lasagna watery.

In a food processor, blend the cottage cheese until it has a creamy, uniform texture.

Transfer this into a mixing bowl and add the remaining ingredients for the "ricotta-style" layer. Mix well. Cover and set aside. You may substitute Ricotta and omit the food processor step. Cottage cheese makes this layer creamier, so I always use it in place of Ricotta.

To make the Pesach "noodles," lightly beat 6 eggs in a medium bowl. Add water and tapioca flour and mix thoroughly until you have a uniform batter. Allow to sit for 3-5 minutes before cooking. Cook the batter into "crepes." This amount of batter will yield approximately 9 "crepes." Heat a small skillet over medium high heat. Use oil or cooking spray as needed. Cook until the batter is no longer runny, then flip to finish cooking the other side. These cook quickly, and only need 1-3 minutes per side.

Once all the "crepes" are cooked, slice them into 2" strips.

Preheat oven to 350°F.

To assemble the lasagna, smear roughly ½ cup of marinara sauce onto the base of a deep 13x9 baking dish.

Line the dish with a layer of the tapioca "noodles." (Use approximately 3 "crepes," sliced)

cont.

Layer all of the roasted vegetables on top of the "noodles."

Spread 1-1½ cups of marinara sauce evenly over the vegetables. (If you use too much, the overall result will be a little too "saucy.")

Evenly spread 2-3 cups of the grated mozzarella over the sauce. (I like an extra cheesy lasagna, but if you'd like to minimize the cheese, feel free to use less.)

Create another layer of "noodles" over the cheese. (Use approximately 3 "crepes," sliced.)

Evenly spread the cottage cheese (or ricotta) mixture over the layer of noodles.

Place another layer of "noodles" over the cottage cheese mixture. (Use approximately 3 "crepes," sliced.)

Spread approximately 1½ cups of marinara sauce over the noodles.

Sprinkle 2-3 cups of mozzarella (or less, to taste) over the sauce.

Top with grated parmesan.

Cover the dish with aluminum foil and bake for 40-45 minutes. Remove foil and bake for an additional 5-10 minutes at 400°F, until the cheese is browned on top.

Allow to cool for 10-15 minutes before slicing and serving.

Serves 8-12

Vegetable Moussaka

During the year, my favorite way to make Moussaka is to use a vegetarian fake ground meat substitute with a traditional dairy bechamel on top. This recipe uses a mushroom blend in place of the meat with a fairly traditional, but chametz-free, bechamel style parmesan sauce. If you want to serve this as a vegetarian option with a fleishig meal, you can make it parve by simply using the roasted cauliflower sauce from the meat Moussaka on page 108 of this book.

Ingredients:

3-4 large Eggplants
4 large Potatoes, peeled and cut into ¼" slices
1-2 Tbs. Olive Oil, plus more for frying eggplant
4 large Portobello Mushrooms, roughly chopped
6 oz. White Mushrooms, roughly chopped
6 oz. Cremini Mushrooms, roughly chopped
1 cup Raw Cashews
1 Parve Beef Flavored Bouillon Cube (or 1 tsp. of any parve soup mix)
1 cup Boiling Water
2 Onions, finely chopped
5 cloves Garlic, minced
1 (15oz.) can Crushed Tomatoes
2 Tbs. Tomato Paste
½ tsp. Cinnamon
¼ tsp. Allspice
3 Tbs. Fresh Flat Leaf Parsley, minced
1 tsp. Oregano
1 tsp. Salt, divided, plus more to taste
½ tsp. Black Pepper
½ cup Red Wine
1-2 tsp. Tapioca Flour (optional)
1 Egg, beaten

Non-Stick Cooking Spray

For the Bechamel Sauce: *To make this dish parve, substitute Cauliflower Sauce from page 108

6 Tbs. Butter
½ cup Tapioca Flour
2 cup Whole Milk
Salt and Pepper to taste
¼-½ tsp. Freshly Grated Nutmeg
6 oz. Parmesan Cheese, grated
2 Egg Yolks

Instructions:

Begin by preparing the cashews. Dissolve 1 Parve Beef Flavored Bouillon cube in 1 cup of boiling water. Add the cashews and soak for 30-45 minutes while you prepare other components of the dish.

To prepare the eggplant, cut off the top and bottom of each and use a vegetable peeler to peel strips down each side, about 1 inch apart. Some people prefer to peel their eggplant entirely, but I find that the dish becomes too mushy without a bit of the skin to give it some structure. Cut each eggplant into ¼" slices.

If you'd like to draw out some of the moisture, at this stage, lay out the eggplant slices on cutting boards lined with paper towels. Sprinkle a bit of salt onto each slice and allow to sit for about 30 minutes. I usually measure about 1 teaspoon of salt into a bowl and use that to limit the total amount that can be sprinkled onto the eggplant. Once the moisture beads, use a paper towel to pat the slices dry. I only do this on one side of each slice. When I have tried salting both sides, the result has just been too salty.

Heat olive oil in a pan over medium high heat. Fry the eggplant slices in batches until they are soft and a bit browned. Remove to a paper towel lined tray to drain while you finish frying the remainder of the eggplant. Set aside until you are ready to assemble the dish.

To prepare the potatoes, bring a large pot of salted water to a boil on the stove. Add the peeled slices and boil for about 5 minutes. Remove from heat and drain. Set aside until you are ready to assemble the dish.

Place the portobello, white and cremini mushrooms into the bowl of a food processor. (You may do this chopping by hand if you don't have an appliance.) Pulse to chop until the mushrooms are finely minced. They should approximate the texture of ground meat. Remove from the food processor and set aside.

Drain the cashews that were soaking and place them in the bowl of the food processor. Pulse until they are crumbled and resemble a ground meat texture. Add the cashews to the mushroom blend.

In a large sauté pan on the stove, heat 1-2 tablespoons of olive oil over medium heat. Add the onions. Cook for about 10-12 minutes until they caramelize a bit.

Add 4 cloves of minced garlic and cook for another 3-4 minutes.

Add the mushroom/cashew blend to the pan and cook until the mushrooms soften. Continue to cook until most of the moisture has cooked off. (approximately 30 minutes.)

Add the crushed tomatoes, tomato paste, cinnamon, allspice, parsley, oregano, pepper and wine. Mix to combine thoroughly. If you'd like a thicker sauce with a bit more chewiness, add 1-2 teaspoons of tapioca flour at this point. Mix well.

Bring to a boil, then reduce heat to a simmer. Cook uncovered for about 45 minutes until the liquid is absorbed.

Taste the sauce and add salt as needed.

Remove from heat and allow to cool a bit.

Mix in the beaten egg once the sauce has cooled to the point that it will not cook the egg.

To make the bechamel sauce, melt the butter in a saucepan over low heat.

Add the tapioca flour and whisk to combine.

Continue whisking and cooking for another 3-4 minutes.

Add 1 cup of milk all at once, and whisk to create a smooth sauce. Try to eliminate any lumps.

Add the remaining 1 cup of milk and whisk to combine. Raise the heat to medium and bring to a low boil.

Continue cooking and whisking as the sauce thickens. It should take about 3-5 minutes.

Reduce heat a bit and add parmesan and ¼ teaspoon nutmeg.

Whisk to combine until the mixture is smooth and heated through.

Taste the sauce and add salt, pepper and additional nutmeg to taste.

Remove from heat and allow to cool a bit.

Whisk in 2 egg yolks once the sauce has cooled to the point that it will not cook them.

Preheat oven to 350°F and assemble the Moussaka.

Grease a 9x11 baking dish with non-stick cooking spray. I have not included matzah meal in this recipe because it has gluten and may bring up issues of gebrochts, but if you eat it, and you'd like to sprinkle some in the bottom of the dish to absorb some of the moisture, that is an option. You may also sprinkle a layer of potato starch in the bottom of the dish if you'd like to absorb some of the liquid, but it is not absolutely necessary.

Create a layer of potato slices that overlap a bit on the bottom of the baking dish. Use about half of the eggplant to create an overlapping layer of slices on top of this. Spread the mushroom sauce on top in an even layer. Layer the remainder of the eggplant on top of the mushroom sauce. Finally, spread the bechamel sauce evenly over the top.

Bake, uncovered, for about 1 hour. Allow to cool a bit before cutting into the dish.

Serves 8-12

Sweet Potato Gnocchi in a Brown Butter Sage Sauce

I have a friend who absolutely loves sweet potatoes, so this recipe is for you, Nicole. Regular potato gnocchi had become a staple for me, and I realized that I could use other starchy vegetables in the same way. The sauce in this dish is incredibly rich, so a little goes a long way. If you are serving it with a fleishig meal, use parve margarine in place of butter. But butter is really the best way to experience this sauce, so I'd suggest making this dish the star of a sophisticated dairy meal.

Ingredients:

1½ cups Sweet Potatoes (about
    3 medium Sweet Potatoes)
1 Egg, lightly beaten, at room
    temperature
1 cup Potato Flour, plus more for
    rolling gnocchi
1 tsp. Salt

For the Sauce:
1 stick Butter or Margarine*
1 clove Garlic, minced
2 Tbs. Fresh Sage, finely
    chopped
¼ tsp. Salt
¼ tsp. Black Pepper

Toasted Pine Nuts, to garnish

Instructions:

Preheat oven to 400°F.

Clean the sweet potatoes, but do NOT peel them. Poke holes in each with a fork or paring knife. Place on a baking sheet and bake for about 45-50 minutes, or until soft.

Allow the sweet potatoes to cool enough to be handled, then peel them with a paring knife. Place the flesh in a large bowl. You should have approximately 1½ cups after roasting and peeling. Mash the flesh with a masher or fork, until there are no large lumps.

Add the egg and mix well.

Add the potato flour and salt and combine thoroughly.

This dough is very soft and can be difficult to roll into gnocchi. I have found that the best option is to cover and refrigerate the dough for at least 4 hours. This makes it much easier to work with. Alternatively, you can simply use 2 spoons or a melon baller to create small bites, approximately the size of pieces of gnocchi. Even if they don't have a traditional gnocchi shape, this will be easier and faster and will taste just as good. Simply drop each one into boiling water as you form it.

If you choose to roll out a traditional gnocchi shape, after the dough has chilled, roll the dough into ¾" strands and cut 1" lengths. I usually do this on a surface covered with parchment paper so that I don't have to use extra potato flour.

Bring a pot of water to boil on the stove. In batches, boil the gnocchi pieces for about 5 minutes. Do not stir. They will float to the top on their own. Remove with a slotted spoon.

This gnocchi is oddly chewy immediately after boiling. As it sits, it becomes less chewy and tastes more like sweet potato.

To make the sauce, melt butter or margarine in a small sauté pan over a medium low heat. Cook for about 12 minutes.

Add the minced garlic and cook for another 2-3 minutes. The sauce should be a bit brown, but not burned.

Stir in sage and cook for another 3 minutes.

Add salt and pepper to taste and serve immediately over sweet potato gnocchi.

Garnish with toasted pine nuts.

*Be sure to use margarine if making this dish parve.

Serves 4-6

Eggplant Parmesan

This may be my favorite food of all time. I love eggplant any way I can get it. Combine that with cheese and it doesn't get any better for me. The thing that I've learned from years of eating bad versions of eggplant parmesan in restaurants (and at home)… is that the most important thing is to avoid thick slices of eggplant. The best version I ever had of this dish was at an Italian restaurant many years ago. The slices of eggplant were shockingly thin, but it made all the difference in the world. I've been trying to replicate it ever since. And this recipe is as close as I've gotten. I've also found that salting the slices and letting some of the water dry out does help a bit, but it is not an absolutely essential step if you want to save some time. It does take time to thoroughly fry all the eggplant, so this will take the better part of an afternoon. Still…to me, totally worth it! The key to this dish is not to over-sauce. Add more sauce or cheese, as desired, but beware of drowning the dish.

Ingredients:

4 large Eggplant
1 cup Marinara Sauce, divided
6 oz. Fontina Cheese slices
8 oz. Mozzarella Cheese,
   shredded, or more to taste
Freshly Grated Parmesan, to taste

Olive oil and salt for frying

Instructions:

I generally use jarred marinara sauce to make this recipe. There are many kosher l'Pesach options that are good, and it saves time. If you prefer making a sauce from scratch, that's great. If you need a recipe, see page 144 in this book.

Remove the ends of each eggplant and use a vegetable peeler to peel strips down the sides of each one, about an inch apart. This breaks up the skin so that the eggplants are easier to eat in the finished dish. Cut each eggplant into 1/4 inch slices.

If you'd like to draw out some of the moisture, at this stage, lay out the eggplant slices on cutting boards lined with paper towels. Sprinkle a bit of salt onto each slice and allow to sit for 20-30 minutes. I usually measure about 1 teaspoon of salt into a bowl and use that to limit the total amount that can be sprinkled onto the eggplant. Once the moisture beads, use a paper towel to pat the slices dry. I only do this on one side of each slice. When I have tried salting both sides, the result has just been too salty.

Heat olive oil in a pan over medium high heat. Fry the eggplant slices in batches. Use a firm spatula to press the slices while they are cooking. The slices are ready when they are completely soft and a bit browned. Remove to a paper towel lined tray to drain while you finish frying the remainder of the eggplant.

To assemble the dish, spread about 1/2 cup of marinara sauce evenly on the bottom of a 9x13 baking dish.

Cover with a layer of 1/2 of the sauteed eggplant.

Add a layer of Fontina cheese. If you'd like an extra cheesy result, top this with additional shredded mozzarella.

Spread about 1/4-1/2 cup of marinara sauce evenly over the cheese. Cover with a layer of the remaining eggplant. Add a layer of Mozzarella cheese. Cover with a layer of freshly grated Parmesan.

Cover with foil, and bake in a 350°F oven for 30-40 minutes. For a crispier top, remove foil for the last 10 minutes of baking.

Serves about 8-10

Smoked Mushroom Stroganoff

Smoking the mushrooms gives this dish something extra that makes it really special. However, it does make it more complicated. And it will smoke up your kitchen. You can absolutely omit the smoking step and simply make a mushroom stroganoff. Alternatively, if you can find a kosher l'Pesach liquid smoke (which I hear does exist, though I've never been able to track it down)...you can also skip the smoking step and just add a bit to the sauce. But if you like smoked flavor, and you're willing to try something totally different in the kitchen, it complements this dish incredibly well.

Ingredients:

4 Tbs. Earl Grey Tea
8 oz. Cremini Mushrooms, chopped
8 oz. White Mushrooms, chopped
5 oz. Shiitake Mushrooms, chopped
1 large Onion, diced
4 cloves Garlic, minced
1 Tbs. Olive Oil
2 Tbs. Butter
$1/3$ cup White Wine
1 cup Vegetable Stock
1-2 Tbs. Potato Starch (depending on how thick you want the Stroganoff to be)
1 cup Sour Cream
Salt and Pepper to taste (about ½-¾ tsp. each)

Italian Flat Leaf Parsley to garnish

Instructions:

To smoke the mushrooms, you will need a pot and a steamer basket with a well fitted lid. Line the pot with 3-4 layers of aluminum foil. Place the earl grey tea in a pile on the foil in the middle of the pot. Put the pot on a burner on the stove set to a medium-high temperature. Put the chopped mushrooms in the steamer basket and place it on top of the pot, uncovered. Watch carefully until you see smoke rise up through the mushrooms (about 5-5 ½ minutes). Cover the basket with a tight fitting lid. Wait 30 seconds, then reduce heat to medium. Smoke for 5 minutes, then remove from heat. Set aside.

In a large pan on the stove, heat the oil and sauté the onion until it begins to brown.

Add butter, garlic and mushrooms and cook until tender.

Add the wine to deglaze the pan, and bring to a simmer. Cook for about 5 minutes.

In a bowl, combine vegetable stock and potato starch. Mix well.

Reduce heat and add the vegetable stock mixture to the pan. Combine thoroughly. Gradually increase heat and cook for 5-10 minutes.

Add sour cream and heat through.

Add salt and pepper to taste.

Serve over mashed potatoes, zoodles or pesach pasta and garnish with chopped parsley.

Serves 4-6

Chilis Rellenos

This is a fun, delicious dairy main course that is not your usual Pesach meal. I like to add dishes that are unexpected to my Pesach menu because, for me, it adds to the festive nature of the week. I am also thrilled to eat anything with a cheese filling. If you make the Tex-Mex Kale salad on page 68 without chicken, it is a great side for this dish.

Ingredients:

6-8 Poblano Peppers
5 large Roma Tomatoes
1 small Yellow Onion, chopped
1 Jalapeño
1 Garlic Bulb
¾ cup Cilantro Leaves
2 Tbs. Olive Oil
2 Tbs. Lime Juice
Salt and Black Pepper to taste

For the Filling:
1½ tsp. Oregano
½ tsp. Paprika
8 oz. Shredded Mozzarella

For the Batter:
3 Eggs, separated, room temperature
¾ tsp. White Vinegar
½ cup Potato Flour

Oil for Frying

Instructions:

After many attempts at removing the seeds from a roasted poblano, I have learned that it is much easier to remove the seeds before cooking these peppers.

Cut a slit about 2/3 of the way around the stem of each poblano. Try to pull the stem back/out a bit without removing it. With a paring knife, gently remove the inner membrane that holds the seeds. Remove any additional seeds from the pepper. Flushing it with a bit of water will usually help dislodge the seeds. It is also fine if you just remove the entire top of the pepper and serve this dish without the stems.

In a 400°F oven, under a broiler or over an open flame on the stove, roast the Poblano peppers, jalapeño and tomatoes. Poke holes in the skin of the jalepeno and tomatoes before roasting so that they do not burst. Cook until they are charred, turning as needed. In the oven it will take about 35-45 minutes. If you roast these in the oven, they can cook alongside the garlic in the next step.

To roast the garlic, rub off any loose skin from the bulb. Carefully slice off the top (pointed) end of the bulb. Each clove should be exposed. Use a small knife to cut off the tips of any cloves that are still encased. Place the garlic in a small baking dish or simply wrap it in foil. (I always just wrap the garlic in some foil. It is the easiest way to roast.) Drizzle with about 1 tsp. olive oil and sprinkle with salt and pepper. Cover the dish (or close up the top of the foil packet). Roast the garlic in a 400°F oven for 30-35 minutes.

Once the Poblano peppers are roasted, place them in a zip-top baggie or sealed foil pouch to cool. The resulting steam will make the skin easier to peel off.

In a skillet over medium heat, sauté the onions in olive oil until they are soft and a bit caramelized. Remove from heat and allow to cool a bit before transferring them to the bowl of a food processor.

Remove the skin, stem and seeds from the jalapeño. (The seeds are spicy, so if you'd like the dish to be hotter, feel free to leave them in.)

Add the skinned jalapeño, the roasted tomatoes and cilantro to the food processor with the onions. Squeeze the roasted pulp of the garlic out of the skin into the food processor, as well.

Blend the vegetables until they are pureed.

Transfer this mixture back to the skillet where the onions were cooked.

Add the lime juice and cook over a medium heat until the sauce thickens a bit. Add salt and pepper to taste.

To make the filling, simply combine the mozzarella, oregano and paprika in a bowl and mix well.

Once the Poblano peppers have cooled, carefully remove the skin from each. Try not to damage the peppers while skinning them.

Stuff each pepper with some of the mozzarella mixture. Set aside.

In the bowl of an electric stand mixer or with a hand mixer, whip the egg whites. Once they are foamy, add the vinegar and continue whipping to stiff peaks.

Add the yolks and whip until a smooth batter forms.

Pour the potato flour into a shallow dish or plate. Carefully roll each stuffed pepper in the potato flour so that they are completely covered.

Then, dip each one into the egg mixture. Spoon the egg mixture over them until they are well coated.

Fry the coated peppers in vegetable oil in a skillet over medium high heat. Cook until golden brown, flipping as needed.

Serve the peppers with plenty of sauce.

Serves 4

Gado Gado

I spent some time in Indonesia a long time ago, so I learned a bit about the local cuisine. One really interesting dish is Gado Gado. It is basically a mixture (it literally means mix mix) of a lot of components that don't seem to go together...but end up creating a delightfully strange harmony. This is a dish that traditionally uses shellfish and about 7 different forms of kitniyot, so it was a challenge to make it kosher for Pesach. It may seem like an odd combination of random ingredients, but they actually come together to make a wonderful parve main dish that is vegetarian friendly. Also, this sauce is fantastic and it goes well over quinoa bowls or as a satay sauce for grilled chicken.

Ingredients:

2 large Portobello Mushrooms
2 Yukon Gold Potatoes, unpeeled
4 Hard Boiled Eggs, peeled
1 cup Red Cabbage, shredded
1 cup Enoki Mushrooms, roughly
    chopped
2 Shallots, sliced
1 cup Asparagus
4 cups Romaine Lettuce, chopped
2 Roma Tomatoes, cut into chunks
2 Persian Cucumbers, diced
1-2 Tbs. Olive Oil
Optional: Nut Crackers to serve with
    the dish

For the Sauce:
2 cups Raw Cashews
6-10 Red Chili Peppers, chopped
10 cloves Garlic, minced
1-2 Tbs. Oil (ideally, Coconut Oil)
1½ cup Coconut Milk
3 Tbs. Tamarind Paste
2 Tbs. Lime Juice
½ -1 cup Water
1 tsp. Sugar
½-1 tsp. Salt, to taste

Instructions:

Begin by preparing vegetables, individually.

Preheat oven to 400°F.

Place the portobellos on a parchment lined baking sheet. Drizzle or brush with olive oil and sprinkle with salt. Cover them with foil and roast for about 30 minutes, or until soft. Slice or cut them into chunks once they cool enough to be touched. Set aside.

Boil the potatoes in salted water, until they are totally cooked through. I prefer to boil them whole, then cut them into wedges. This does take longer, so if you'd like to save time, you may cut them up first. If you pre-cut them, be careful when removing them from the water so that the pieces retain their integrity. Once they are boiled and cut into wedges, set aside.

Bring a pot of salted water to a boil and blanch the shredded cabbage. Cook for 30 seconds to a maximum of 2 minutes. Remove from water and set aside.

Steam the asparagus and cut the stalks into 1" pieces. Set aside.

Hard boil and peel the eggs. Cut them into wedges and set aside.

In a small skillet, heat olive oil over a medium heat. Sauté the enoki mushrooms until they are cooked through. Remove from the pan and set aside.

In the same pan, adding additional oil if necessary, cook shallots until they are soft and a bit caramelized.

To make the sauce, roast the cashews in a non-stick skillet over medium heat for about 6-8 minutes. Shake or stir the pan often and do NOT allow the cashews to burn. Remove from the skillet and set aside.

In the same skillet, heat 1-2 tablespoons of coconut oil (or any other cooking oil). Add the chilis and garlic and cook until they soften and brown a bit.

Place the cashews, chilis and garlic into the bowl of a food processor or blender. Add about 1 cup of the coconut milk and ½ cup water and blend until a smooth paste forms.

Transfer this mixture to a sauce pan on the stove and add tamarind paste, lime juice, sugar, salt and the remainder of the coconut milk. If you prefer a thicker sauce, you may limit the amount of coconut milk you add. If you prefer a thinner sauce, you can add additional coconut milk and/or water. Mix well to combine thoroughly and heat over a low flame. Adjust salt to taste.

Divide all of the ingredients evenly into bowls for each person. Add warm sauce to each dish and garnish with nut crackers

Serves 2-3

Shakshuka-touille

I've been trying to love shakshuka for a long time. It seems like the egg whites are always too runny, and even if they are well cooked, the flavors are a bit boring. I am always disappointed. Until now. This recipe is a combination of Shakshuka and Ratatouille. The additional vegetables and tarragon give the dish a much more interesting flavor, but the key is to cook the egg whites long enough to be firm while the yolks are still soft. The leftover sauce is also great served with mashed potatoes or quinoa.

Ingredients:

3-4 Tbs. Olive Oil, divided
1 large Eggplant, cut into cubes
1 Yellow Onion, diced
1 Red Bell Pepper, chopped
1 Zucchini, chopped
6 cloves Garlic, minced
2 tsp. Paprika
1 tsp. Turmeric
½ tsp. Salt (plus more to taste)
½ tsp. Black Pepper
pinch of Cayenne Pepper
   (optional)
1 (28 oz.) can Diced Tomatoes
1/3 cup Parsley, chopped
2 Tbs. Fresh Tarragon, chopped
4-6 Whole Eggs (depending on
   size of pan)

Optional: 1-2 Tbs. Kalamata
   Olives, chopped for garnish

Instructions:

Heat 1-2 tbs. olive oil over a medium high heat in a large sauté pan or Dutch oven. Sauté eggplant until soft and a bit charred. Set aside.

Add another 1-2 tbs. olive oil to the same pan, and cook the onions until they caramelize. (about 10-12 minutes).

Add bell pepper and zucchini and cook until soft.

Add garlic and dry spices and cook for another 2 minutes.

Add the canned tomatoes. Cook until the juice from the tomatoes reduces and the sauce thickens a bit.

Return the eggplant to the pan and bring to a simmer.

Once simmering, use a spatula to create a small hole in the sauce for each egg. Add the eggs one at a time after cracking them open and checking for blood spots.

Reduce heat to medium low. Cover and cook for 5-10 minutes until the eggs reached desired firmness.

Sprinkle parsley and tarragon on top and add salt to taste. Serve hot.

Garnish with Kalamata olives (optional).

Serves 4

Quinoa Bowls

An Introduction to Quinoa Bowls:

Quinoa bowls are one of my go-to staples on Pesach. They can be made from whatever you like to eat, and whatever happens to be lying around the pantry. They can stand alone, or they can be one course in a larger meal. You could even plan a meal around a build-your-own-quinoa-bowl bar where everyone can choose their preferred ingredients. They're also a great option for vegetarians or vegans because quinoa is a Pesach-friendly protein source. There are essentially no rules, but I will share a few guidelines.

In general, quinoa bowls include:

-a scoop of cooked quinoa
-some kind of leafy green (Kale, Romaine, Arugula, Spinach, etc.)
-a protein (Chicken, Fish, Egg, Cheese, etc.)
-fresh, roasted and/or pickled vegetables (cucumber, peppers, olives, carrots, etc.)
-fresh and/or dried fruit and/or nuts (pomegranate seeds, raisins, apples, etc.)
-fresh herbs (basil, mint, cilantro, etc.)
-some kind of dressing or sauce (pesto, chimichurri, hot honey mayo, ranch, etc.)

The options are limitless for mixing and matching, within the boundaries of kashrut, of course.

How to cook quinoa   PARVE

For years, I struggled to cook quinoa properly. It was usually completely over cooked, mushy and virtually inedible. Thankfully, I stumbled on a foolproof method several years ago, and my quinoa has turned out reliably well ever since!

The first step to making great quinoa is rinsing the quinoa. Use a fine strainer (or even a bowl and your hand in a pinch). Rinse the quinoa very well with cold water. This removes a natural compound called Saponin that creates a bitter taste. If you've ever had plain quinoa that tasted bitter...it was very likely because the person cooking it did not rinse it first. This makes a big difference.

The ratio for quinoa to water is 1 part quinoa to 2 parts water. You can also use vegetable or chicken broth instead of water to give it more flavor. I often add a bit of vegetable stock powder to the water before boiling.

Combine quinoa and cold water in a pot on the stove. Bring to a boil, uncovered. Once it has boiled, turn down the heat so that the mixture simmers, but don't cover it. Allow to cook until the water has been absorbed. (This takes about 15-20 minutes for 1 cup of quinoa. It will take longer if you are making a larger amount). Once the quinoa reaches this point, turn off the heat and cover the pot with a well-fitting lid for 5 minutes. This will allow the steam to finish cooking the quinoa. Fluff with a fork.

One cup of uncooked quinoa makes roughly 3 cups of cooked quinoa.

Greek Salad Quinoa Bowl

Ingredients: (Per Bowl)

1 cup Cooked Quinoa
2 cups Romaine Lettuce, chopped
½ cup Persian Cucumbers, cubed
½ cup Cherry Tomatoes, halved or
    quartered
¼ cup Red Onion, finely sliced
⅓ cup Kalamata Olives, pitted and
    chopped
¼ cup Pepperoncinis, chopped
1-2 oz. Feta Cheese, crumbled
Greek Yogurt Feta Dressing, to taste

Greek Yogurt Feta Dressing:
2 oz. Feta Cheese
1 cup Greek Yogurt
2 Tbs. Lemon Juice
zest of 1 Lemon
1 clove Garlic, minced
¼ cup Italian Flat Leaf Parsley,
    chopped
Salt and Pepper to taste.

Instructions:

To make the dressing, combine Feta and Greek Yogurt in a bowl. Mix thoroughly. Add lemon juice, lemon zest, garlic and parsley and mix to combine. Season with salt and pepper, to taste.

Place a scoop of quinoa in a bowl and cover with the remaining toppings. Drizzle dressing over the top and serve.

Beet Goat Cheese Quinoa Bowl

Ingredients: (Per Bowl)

1 cup Cooked Quinoa
2 cups Arugula, roughly chopped
1-2 oz. Creamy Goat Cheese
¾ cup Eggplant, cubed and
    sauteed until charred
1-2 Tbs. Red Onion, finely chopped
½ cup Beets, chopped (canned
    beets are fine, and even raw
    sliced beets work!)
½ cup Fresh Figs, (or ¼ cup dried)
    chopped
1 small Avocado, diced
¼ cup Walnuts, chopped
Balsamic Vinaigrette, to taste

Instructions:

Place a scoop of quinoa in the bowl and cover with the remaining toppings. Drizzle dressing over the top and serve.

Spinach Egg Quinoa Bowl

Ingredients: (Per Bowl)

1 cup Cooked Quinoa
2 Hard Boiled Eggs, peeled and
   chopped
2 cups Baby Spinach, roughly
   chopped
½ cup Asparagus, steamed and cut
   into 1" pieces
1 small Avocado, diced
⅓ cup Radishes, shredded or finely
   chopped
¼ cup Green Olives, chopped
¼ cup Walnuts, chopped
1-2 Tbs. Pomegranate Seeds
   (optional)
Harissa Dressing to taste

Harissa Dressing
⅓ cup Olive Oil
2-3 Tbs. Red Wine Vinegar
2 Tbs. Harissa
1 clove Garlic, minced
1 tsp. Honey
Salt to taste

Instructions:

To make the dressing, combine all ingredients. It is easiest to use a jar with a lid and shake well to mix. You may also whisk to combine in a bowl. Adjust seasoning to taste.

Place a scoop of quinoa in a bowl and cover with the remaining toppings. Drizzle dressing over the top and serve.

Kale Chicken Quinoa Bowl

Ingredients: (Per Bowl)

1 cup Cooked Quinoa
2-4 oz. Roasted or Grilled Chicken,
    sliced or shredded
2 cups Kale, shredded and
    massaged
½ cup Roasted Sweet Potatoes,
    cubed
½ cup Granny Smith Apple, peeled
    and diced
¼ cup Toasted Pecans, chopped
2-3 Tbs. Dried Cranberries
Spicy Honey Mayo Dressing,
    to taste

Spicy Honey Mayo Dressing:
½ cup Mayonnaise
1 tsp. Apple Cider Vinegar
2 Tbs. Honey
¼ tsp. Garlic Powder
½ tsp. Paprika
¼ tsp. cayenne (or more, to taste)
Salt to taste

Instructions:

To make the dressing, combine all ingredients in a bowl and mix well. Adjust seasoning to taste.

Place a scoop of quinoa in a bowl and cover with the remaining toppings. Drizzle dressing over the top and serve.

Pan-Seared Salmon Quinoa Bowl

Ingredients: (Per Bowl)

1 cup Cooked Quinoa
2-4 oz. Pan-Seared Salmon
1-2 cups Mixed Greens, chopped
¼ cup Red Bell Pepper, diced
¼ Shallot, finely chopped
1 cup Terra Chips
1-2 Tbs. Jalapeño, seeds removed,
    finely chopped
¼ cup Mango, finely diced
¼ cup Pineapple, finely diced
2 tsp. Lime Juice
zest of 1 Lime
1 Tbs. Fresh Mint, finely chopped
¼ cup Cilantro, finely chopped
Balsamic Vinaigrette, to taste

Instructions:

In a small bowl, combine pineapple, mango, jalapeño, lime juice, zest and salt to taste. Set aside.

Place a scoop of quinoa in a bowl and cover with the mixed greens, salmon, red bell pepper, shallot and terra chips. Add some (or all) of the pineapple-mango mixture. Top with mint and cilantro. Drizzle dressing over the top and serve.

Grilled Chicken Quinoa Bowl

Ingredients: (Per Bowl)

1 cup Cooked Quinoa
2-4 oz. Grilled Chicken, sliced or
   shredded
1 cup Arugula, chopped
½ cup Roasted or Steamed
   Broccoli, chopped
½ cup Red Cabbage, shredded
¼ cup Pickled Carrots (see recipe
   below)
1-2 Tbs. Fresh Basil, chopped
1-2 Tbs. Fresno Peppers, chopped
   (Optional)

Cilantro-Cashew Dressing, to taste
Salt and Pepper, to taste

Pickled Carrots:
2-3 medium Carrots, peeled and
   shredded
1 cup White Wine Vinegar
3 Tbs. Sugar
½ tsp. Salt

Cilantro-Cashew Dressing:
²/₃ cup Grapeseed Oil
3 Tbs. Cashew Butter,
2-3 Tbs. Apple Cider Vinegar,
2 Tbs. Lime Juice
¾ cup Cilantro Leaves
½ tsp. Ginger Powder
½ tsp. Garlic Powder
pinch of Cayenne
¼ tsp. Salt

Instructions:

To make the pickled carrots, begin by peeling and shredding 2-3 medium carrots. Set aside in a heat proof bowl.

In a small pot on the stove, combine white wine vinegar, sugar and salt. Bring to a simmer and mix until all of the sugar and salt are totally dissolved.

Remove from heat and pour over the shredded carrots in the bowl. Allow to sit for about 1 hour. Drain. Store any leftovers that will not be used in the quinoa bowl in the refrigerator.

To make the Cilantro-Cashew dressing, combine all ingredients in a food processor or blender. Blend until the dressing is totally smooth. Adjust seasoning to taste.

Place a scoop of quinoa in a bowl and cover with the remaining toppings. Drizzle dressing over the top and serve.

Sauces and Staples

Alfredo Sauce

Alfredo sauce is delicious with gnocchi or Pesach pasta. It can be a vegetarian main course alone (especially if you add sauteed mushrooms), or you can add baked or grilled salmon. Depending on how thick you'd like the sauce to be, it can be made with or without a tapioca flour slurry.

Ingredients:

½ cup Butter
3 cloves Garlic, minced (use 1-2 cloves if you prefer less garlicky flavor.)
1½ cups Half & Half
1½ - 2 cups Parmesan Cheese, freshly grated
Salt and Pepper to taste
Italian Parsley, chopped, to garnish

Optional: (for a thicker sauce)
1 tsp. Tapioca Flour
1 Tbs. Water

Instructions:

Melt ½ cup of butter in a pan over medium high heat. Add garlic and sauté for 2-3 minutes.

Add Half & Half and cook for about 15 minutes, stirring frequently. (A whisk works best to stir this sauce.)

Add parmesan cheese and heat through, whisking to combine.

If you'd like the sauce to be thicker, reduce heat and make a slurry. In a small bowl, combine 1 tsp. of tapioca flour with 1 Tbs. of water and mix well. Let the sauce cool a bit before you add this, or it will cook the tapioca flour into a pancake.

Once the sauce has cooled a bit, add the slurry and whisk well to combine thoroughly. Gradually increase the heat to allow the sauce to thicken.

Cook for another 5-8 minutes, stirring frequently.

Add salt and pepper to taste.

Garnish with parsley. Serve over gnocchi, zoodles or Pesach pasta.

Serves 4

Pictured with zoodles

Marinara Sauce

Before I started working on this cookbook, I would never make pasta sauce during Pesach. With all of the other work that goes into food prep, and all of the other dishes that I can't buy pre-made, it seemed unnecessary. However, I wanted to include a basic recipe for people who might not have access to a jar from a kosher market. Learning to make this sauce completely changed my opinion. This homemade sauce is actually very simple to make, and the flavor is so far beyond anything you can buy in a jar, that I now use it exclusively.

A traditional marinara sauce is simple and doesn't have the extras that a lot of people add nowadays. Added ingredients like oregano, balsamic vinegar, red wine, tomato paste and sugar are fairly common, but I wanted to share the classic version. You can always add the bells and whistles to taste.

Ingredients:

2 Tbs. Olive Oil
6 cloves Garlic, minced
28 oz. can of Crushed
   Tomatoes
2 Tbs. Fresh Basil, finely
   chopped
Pinch of Crushed Red pepper
   Flakes
Salt and Black Pepper to taste

Instructions:

Heat the olive oil in a sauce pan over medium heat. Add garlic and cook for 3-5 minutes. Do not allow garlic to turn brown.

Add tomatoes, crushed red pepper flakes, salt and pepper. Simmer for 1 hour. The flavors develop with time, so don't skimp by trying to cook this for 30 minutes.

Add basil. Mix thoroughly and remove from heat. Adjust seasoning to taste.

Serve over gnocchi, zoodles, pesach pasta or in any dish that calls for marinara sauce.

Pictured with Gnocchi.

Yield: About 2 ½ cups

Parve Alfredo Sauce

This is a great sauce to serve as a vegetarian option with gnocchi, zoodles or pesach pasta at a fleishig meal. Add grilled chicken or salmon for a classic chicken alfredo. I make two different nut creams at Pesach...one based on pine nuts, and the other based on cashews. Depending on the nuts available in your area, either can work, but I think this recipe is MUCH better if you use pine nut cream. (See recipe on page 152.) I also love to add sauteed mushrooms to this sauce.

Ingredients:

¼ cup Margarine
3 cloves Garlic, minced
2 Tbs. Tapioca Flour
½ cup Vegetable Broth, divided
1 cup Pine Nut Cream (See
   recipe on page 152.)
Salt to taste*

Parsley to garnish

Instructions:

Make sure that you have the pine nut cream prepared before starting this recipe.

Melt the margarine in a sauté pan over medium heat. Add garlic and cook for about 3 minutes, stirring constantly. Reduce heat to low.

In a small bowl, combine the tapioca flour with 2 Tbs. of the broth and mix well to make a slurry. Add the remainder of the broth to this slurry and mix well to combine.

Once the margarine and garlic have cooled a bit on the stove, gradually add the broth/tapioca flour mixture, stirring constantly. (If you add the mixture when the margarine is too hot, it can cook the tapioca before everything is mixed together. I made this mistake once and got a tapioca pancake.)

Add the pine nut cream and continue stirring to create a cohesive sauce. Gradually increase the heat to allow the sauce to thicken.

Add salt and pepper to taste and heat to desired consistency. The sauce will also thicken a bit as it cools.

Serve over gnocchi, zoodles or Pesach pasta with chicken or salmon. Garnish with parsley.

Pictured with gnocchi.

*I use as little as 1/8 tsp or as much as ½ tsp depending on what type of broth I use and whether the margarine was salted.

Serves 4

Pesto

PARVE

It feels nearly impossible to write an official recipe for pesto because it is a dish that really should always be made to taste. I still never measure anything when I make it...so I hope you will use this recipe only as a guideline. Adjust everything to your own preference.

Ingredients:

4 cups Fresh Basil Leaves,
   loosely packed
1/3 cup Pine Nuts
3-4 cloves Garlic, minced
Salt (start with about ½ tsp. and
   adjust to taste)
1/3 cup Olive Oil

Yield: about 1 cup

Instructions:

Combine ingredients in the bowl of a food processor. Blend until desired texture is reached.

Adjust salt and garlic to taste. Add extra olive oil for a thinner consistency.

Serve over gnocchi, pesach pasta or zoodles. Use as a dip, spread or salad dressing.

Pictured with gnocchi.

Mushroom White Wine Sauce over Gnocchi

PARVE

I started making this sauce to go with gnocchi just because it is so easy. It is also lighter than an alfredo sauce, so it's a nice option that captures the richness and umami of mushrooms without the heaviness of a cream sauce.

Ingredients:

2 Tbs. Margarine
2 Tbs. Olive Oil
2 Shallots, minced
8 oz. White Mushrooms, sliced
5 oz. Shiitake Mushrooms, sliced
6 cloves Garlic, minced
½ cup White Wine
¼-½ cup Vegetable Stock
   (Optional)
Salt and Black Pepper, to taste
Cayenne Pepper, to taste
   (Optional)

Serves 4-6

Instructions:

Heat the margarine and olive oil in a skillet over medium heat. Sauté the shallots and garlic until they soften and begin to brown.

Add the mushrooms and sprinkle with a bit of salt. Cook until the mushrooms release their juices and soften.

Add wine and cook for about 10 minutes. If you want a thinner sauce, add vegetable stock until you reach desired consistency.

Add salt, pepper and cayenne to taste.

Serve over gnocchi (see recipe on page 95).

Gribiche Sauce

This is a cold sauce that is wonderful over chicken, fish or vegetables, but my favorite way to serve it is over roasted potatoes. There are two ways to make this sauce. It can either be more of a puree made in a food processor, or a slightly chunkier mixture that is made by hand. I prefer the latter, so this recipe does not call for the ingredients to be pureed. If you'd like a more uniform texture, just use a food processor to blend to your ideal consistency.

Ingredients:

2 Hard Boiled Eggs, peeled
1 ½ Tbs. Horseradish Mayonnaise (Chrayonnaise)
¼ cup Grapeseed Oil
½ Tbs. White Wine Vinegar
1 Tbs. Green Olives, finely chopped
1 Tbs. Israeli Pickles, finely chopped
1 Tbs. Italian Flat-Leaf Parsley, chopped
½ Tbs. Fresh Tarragon, chopped
¼ tsp. Salt (plus more to taste)

Instructions:

Cut open the hard boiled eggs. Place the yolks in a small bowl, and set aside the whites.

Add the oil to the bowl with the yolks and mix well to form a thick paste. To this, add the Chrayonnaise and White Wine Vinegar. Mix well.

Chop the egg whites that had been set aside. (this can be a fine or coarse chop, depending on your preference.) Add these chopped egg whites, along with the remaining ingredients to the egg yolk mixture.

Mix thoroughly.

Adjust seasoning to taste.

Serve over Roasted Potatoes, Chicken, Fish or Vegetables.

Serves about 4

Chimichurri Sauce

Chimichurri sauce is an easy, versatile sauce that can enhance almost anything. It can serve as a marinade, a baste or a sauce for meats or vegetables. I have even put leftover sauce on eggs in the morning, and it's delicious. It is traditionally associated with grilled meat or steak, and it is best used by basting the meat while it's cooking, or spooning it onto the cooked meat while it is resting. The key to this recipe is using fresh oregano, so it won't be the same if you try to substitute the dried spice. I chop the oregano very finely before measuring.

Ingredients:

½ cup Olive Oil
2 Tbs. Red Wine Vinegar
¾ cup Italian Parsley
3 cloves Garlic, minced
1 small Jalapeño (about
    ¼ cup), chopped, seeds
    removed
2 tsp. Fresh Oregano, chopped
½ tsp. Salt (plus more to taste)
¼ tsp. Black pepper (plus more
    to taste)

Instructions:

Place parsley, garlic, jalapeno and oregano in a food processor. Pulse until the herbs are chopped well, but not pureed.

Add oil, vinegar, salt and pepper and pulse just until well combined.

Adjust seasoning to taste.

Cover and place in refrigerator for at least 2 hours. Overnight is even better.

Use as a baste or sauce with grilled meats, chicken, fish or vegetables. It also goes well on portobello mushrooms.

Yield: about 1 cup

Carrot Bacon

I created this recipe to serve as a substitute for the vegetarian soy bacon that I use in certain dishes during the year. It is primarily intended to be used in the dairy Cobb salad on page 73, but it can be added to any number of dishes or salads. It goes well with eggs at breakfast or as a CLT (Carrot-Bacon, Lettuce, Tomato Sandwich) on Pesach bread.

Ingredients:

2-3 Large Carrots

2 Tbs. Grapeseed Oil
¼ tsp. Salt
¼ tsp. Black Pepper
¼ tsp. Paprika
¼ tsp. Garlic Powder
1 Tbs. Maple Syrup
½ Tbs. Apple Cider Vinegar

Instructions:

Make a marinade by combining all of the ingredients, except the carrots, in a bowl. Whisk to combine.

Peel the carrots and slice them in half lengthwise. Use a vegetable peeler to careful create wide strips starting with the widest flat (middle) part of the carrot.

Place the carrot strips in the bowl of marinade. Make sure that all of the carrots are well coated. Soak for at least 20-30 minutes.

Preheat oven to 350°F.

Line a baking sheet with parchment paper and spread the carrot strips onto it. Cook for 10-15 minutes, flipping the strips halfway through. Be careful not to let them burn, but do allow them to get a bit charred on the edges. This adds a little smokiness.

If you cook the carrots for about 15 minutes, they will be very crunchy. At 10-12 minutes, they retain a bit of chewiness.

Serves about 4

Parve Pesach Sour Cream: Pine Nut Based

Most of the good parve sour cream substitutes that I use during the year are not kosher for Passover, so I created two versions based on nuts. You can use either of these in recipes that require a parve sour cream alternative, or as a base for salad dressings, dips or any place you'd use sour cream. I have noticed that some of the recipes in this book are better with either the pine nut cream or the cashew cream, so if possible, use the recommended option. However, based on your taste, ingredient availability, cost, etc., use whichever cream is best for you.

Ingredients:

1 cup Raw Pine Nuts
2 cups Hot Water for soaking nuts
   (reserve some water to
   incorporate into the recipe)
1 Tbs. Apple Cider Vinegar
1 tsp. Lemon Juice
Salt to taste (about ½ tsp.)

Instructions:

Soak pine nuts in hot or boiling water for 1 hour.

Drain the water from the nuts, but reserve about 3/4 cup to incorporate into the recipe.

Place the pine nuts, ¼ cup of the reserved soaking water, apple cider vinegar and lemon juice into a food processor or blender. Blend until smooth.

Add salt to taste and blend.

At this point, the cream is probably a bit thick. I always start with ¼ cup of water, then blend and add more as needed to reach the desired consistency. For a thinner cream, use closer to ½ cup of water total. If you are using the cream in a recipe that will be cooked, remember that the cream will thicken as it heats.

Yield: about 1 ½ cups

Parve Pesach Sour Cream: Cashew Based

PARVE

Ingredients:

1 cup Raw Cashews
2 cups Boiling Water for soaking
  nuts (reserve some water to
  incorporate into the recipe)
¼ cup Coconut Cream
1 tsp. Lemon Juice
1 Tbs. Apple Cider Vinegar
Salt to taste (about ½ tsp.)

Instructions:

Soak cashews in boiling water for at least one hour. (I have let the nuts soak up to 4 hours, but 1 hour is sufficient if the water is boiling.)

Drain the cashews, reserving about ¾ cup of the water to incorporate into the recipe.

Place the cashews, ¼ cup of the reserved soaking water, coconut cream, apple cider vinegar and lemon juice into a food processor or blender. Blend until smooth.

Add salt to taste and blend.

If the cream is too thick, add 1-2 Tbs. of the reserved water and blend. Continue adding water and blending until desired consistency is reached. The key to this cream is blending it until it is really smooth. For a bit more tang, add a little more apple cider vinegar and blend until smooth.

Yield: About 1⅓ cups

Accompaniments

Quinoa Crust Goat Cheese Asparagus Quiche

I am including this as a complete recipe, but I almost listed the crust as a dish by itself. The crust works with such a wide variety of savory or sweet fillings, that the number of ways you can use it is nearly limitless. You can follow this recipe, or use entirely different vegetables to fill your crust. I like to add parmesan to the crust because I think it helps it hold together and improves the flavor...but it will work without the cheese, so you can make the crust parve and serve it with a meat meal. It would even be possible to use non-dairy cream alternatives and create a totally parve quiche style dish, so feel free to experiment.

Ingredients:

For the crust:
2 cups of Cooked Quinoa (cook the quinoa before measuring out 2 cups.)
2 Eggs, lightly beaten
1/3 cup Grated Parmesan
1/2 tsp. Salt
1/4 tsp. Black Pepper
Non-Stick Cooking Spray

For the Quiche Filling:
2 Eggs, lightly beaten
1 cup Half & Half
1/2 tsp. Salt
1/4 tsp. Black Pepper

For the Vegetable/Cheese Layer:
1 Tbs. Olive Oil
1 Portobello Mushroom, finely chopped
1 bulb Garlic, roasted
1 cup Asparagus, cut into 3/4" pieces
2-3 oz. Smooth Goat Cheese

Instructions:

Preheat oven to 375°F.

To make the crust, combine the quinoa, eggs, parmesan, salt and pepper in a bowl and mix thoroughly. Spray a pie pan or similar dish with non-stick cooking spray. Pour the mixture into the pan and press it into the sides and bottom, creating a pie crust shape. The easiest way to get an even base is to use a flat bottomed glass or measuring cup to press the crust into place.

Bake for 18-20 minutes at 375°F, and allow to cool before filling.

To roast the garlic, rub off any loose skin on the garlic bulb. Carefully slice off the top (pointed) end of the bulb. Each clove should be exposed. Use a small knife to cut off the tips of any cloves that are still encased. Place the garlic in a small baking dish or simply wrap it in foil. Drizzle with about 1 tsp. olive oil and sprinkle with salt and pepper. Cover the dish with foil (or close up the top of the foil packet). Roast the garlic in a 400°F oven for 30-35 minutes.

Heat 1 tablespoon of olive oil in a skillet over a medium high heat on the stove. Cook the portobello and asparagus until they are tender but not mushy.

Toss the portobello, asparagus and roasted garlic in a bowl so that they are well combined.

Preheat the oven to 350°F

Once the crust is slightly cool, crumble or spread the goat cheese into an even layer on the bottom. Cover this with the mushroom/asparagus mixture.

To make the quiche filling, whisk together the eggs, half & half, salt and pepper. Pour this over the vegetable layer to fill the crust. Bake at 350°F for 45-50 minutes until the quiche is set.

Allow to cool before slicing. Serve warm or room temperature.

*It is important NOT to use a tart pan for this crust if you are using the quiche filling. The crust will not be totally liquid tight, so when the filling is cooking, a bit will seep into the crust and pan that encloses it. A pan with separate sides and bottom will leak.

Serves 8

Carrot Tartare

This dish is meant to be a layered plated appetizer or side, but it can also be mixed together and served almost like a salad. If you cannot find capers that are kosher for Pesach in your area, substitute green olives.

Ingredients:

2 large Carrots, peeled and chopped
3 Tbs. Horseradish Mayonnaise (Chrayonnaise)
1-2 tsp. Anchovies, minced
½ small Shallot, minced
3 Tbs. Capers, minced (substitute Green Olives if unavailable)
1 Tbs. Israeli Pickles, minced
1 tsp. Lemon Juice, plus extra to mix with Avocado topping
1 tsp. Grapeseed or Avocado Oil
Salt and Black Pepper, to taste

Optional: Dash of Worcestershire
   Sauce, to taste, if available in your area for Pesach

2 Avocados, cubed
1 cup Arugula or Micro Greens

Instructions:

In a food processor, pulse the carrots until they are uniformly small and resemble ground beef.

In a mixing bowl, combine Chrayonnaise, anchovies, shallot, capers, pickles, lemon juice and oil. Add the carrots and mix well. Add salt and pepper (and Worcestershire sauce if using), and adjust seasoning to taste.

In a separate bowl, mix avocado cubes with a dash of lemon juice, salt and pepper. Adjust seasoning to taste.

To create a layered appetizer, place a ring mold* in the center of the plate. Scoop some of the avocado mixture into the mold. Use a fork to press it down into a uniform layer. Next, scoop some of the carrot mixture on top of the avocado. Press down with fork. Gently remove the ring mold and top with arugula or micro greens. Repeat for each plate. Alternatively, you may follow this layering pattern in one large bowl to be shared, or even mix it all together like a salad.

*You do not need to use a ring mold to make this work as an individually plated appetizer. Simply place a scoop of the avocado mixture onto a plate. Flatten the top a bit so that it will be a sturdy base for the carrot mixture. Place a scoop of the carrot mixture on top. Top with arugula/greens. It may not look quite as neat as it would with a ring mold, but it is an elegant way to plate this dish if you don't have a mold.

Serves 4-6

Mushroom Rosemary Soufflé

Many people shy away from soufflés. They have a reputation for being fussy and not worth the effort. But, actually, they are relatively easy to make and more forgiving than they are reputed to be. At Pesach, they are a great option because they work well without chametz. They are unique and versatile which adds to the special nature of a chol hamoed breakfast or lunch. I love to cook in ramekins at Pesach, and it's worth investing in a set because they are affordable and have myriad uses. But you can also make one large soufflé in a traditional large dish. I also recommend using a French whisk for this recipe if you do not have an electric stand or hand mixer.

Ingredients:

4 Tbs. Butter, divided (plus
    additional for preparing dishes)
2 Tbs. Parmesan, grated
3 Tbs. Potato Starch
1 cup Whole Milk
½ tsp. Salt
¼ tsp. Pepper
4 Egg Yolks
5 Egg Whites (cold)
1 tsp. White Vinegar
3 oz. Gruyere, grated (Substitute
    Swiss Cheese if you cannot
    access kosher Gruyere)
3 Tbs. Chevre or Smooth Goat
    Cheese
4 oz. Cremini Mushrooms, finely
    chopped
1 Tbs. Olive Oil
2-3 Sprigs Fresh Rosemary

Instructions:

Begin by preparing the dishes. Grease each ramekin (or a large soufflé dish) with butter. Add some grated parmesan to each dish. Move the dish around to allow the parmesan to coat the sides and bottom of the dish well. Pour excess parmesan into additional ramekins until they are all well coated. Wipe the top portion of each dish to the rim so that the top edge is clean. Place the prepared dishes in the refrigerator to chill while you prepare the batter.

In a sauté pan over medium heat, melt 1 tablespoon of butter and 1 tablespoon of olive oil. Once the oil is hot, add the rosemary and cook for 2 minutes. Add the mushrooms and cook until they are soft. (About 5 more minutes.) Remove from heat, discard the rosemary and set the mushrooms aside.

In a sauce pan over medium low heat, melt 3 tablespoons of butter. Add the potato starch, whisking constantly.

Slowly add the milk, whisking constantly to avoid lumps. Bring to a simmer and allow to cook until the mixture thickens. (About 3-5 minutes).

Add salt and pepper, whisk thoroughly.

Remove the mixture from heat and transfer it to a large mixing bowl. Allow it to cool slightly, then whisk in egg yolks, goat cheese and mushrooms. Set aside.

In a large mixing bowl with a hand mixer (or French whisk) or the bowl of an electric mixer, combine egg whites and vinegar and whip to stiff peaks.

Fold 1/3 of the egg whites into the milk/yolk/mushroom mixture.

Fold the gruyere into this mixture. Finally, gently fold in the remainder of the egg whites until just combined.

Place batter in refrigerator to chill for 20 minutes.

Preheat oven to 375°F.

Remove prepared ramekins from the refrigerator and arrange them on a baking sheet. Pour batter into each dish, up to the inner ridge line.

Bake in the oven for 20-25 minutes (for ramekins) or 40-43 minutes (for a large soufflé dish) If you prefer a looser soufflé, cook for a bit less time. If you prefer a firmer, more well done result, cook a bit longer.

The soufflés fall a bit as they cool. They also firm up a bit. Serve in ramekins or slide a table knife around the edges to loosen and pop them out to plate them.

Yields 6 (7 oz.) ramekins or 1 large (1 ½ Qt.) soufflé

Chawanmushi

PARVE

Chawanmushi is a delicate, savory egg custard that makes an elegant breakfast. It is a Japanese dish, so there are a lot of kitniyot based ingredients in traditional recipes. I have modified this recipe so that it can be made with ingredients that are accessible in most kosher markets. The only thing that may be a bit challenging to find are dried shiitake mushrooms. However, they are easy to make for yourself! Although it will not be the same, if you cannot get dried shiitakes, you can substitute kosher l'Pesach imitation soy sauce.

Ingredients:

6 Dried Shiitake Mushrooms
½ cup Hot Water
½ Carrot, peeled
1 large White Mushroom
1 Scallion
1 Radish
1 large Egg
½ tsp. Cooking Sherry
½ tsp. White Wine Vinegar
¼ tsp. Salt

Optional: a pinch of cayenne pepper

Instructions:

To dehydrate fresh shiitakes, simply place them on a baking sheet in a 175° F oven. Cook for about 4 hours, turning them halfway through. Allow them to sit uncovered on a counter until you are ready to use them. This may be done in advance, as they can sit and continue to dry for several days.

Make dashi by soaking the dried shiitake mushrooms in ½ cup of hot (not boiling) water. The dashi will have a stronger flavor with a longer soak time. Soak for a minimum of 20 minutes or up to 24 hours.

Slice the carrot, white mushroom, scallion and radish into moderately thin slices. These vegetables will be steamed in the egg, so if the slices are very thick, they will not be as soft. If they are cut too small, they will not have much texture.

In a bowl, whisk the egg. Add the soaking liquid (dashi) from the shiitake/water mixture. Add sherry, vinegar and salt and whisk. Strain this mixture to eliminate any thick clumps. Add a pinch of cayenne at this point if you want to give the Chawanmushi a little kick.

Arrange the sliced vegetables into ramekins. Pour egg mixture over vegetables. It is OK if the egg does not cover the vegetables. Cover each ramekin with aluminum foil.

In a large lidded sauté pan or shallow pot, add enough water so that it comes to a depth of halfway up the cups. (I put the cups in at this point to determine how much water I need in the pan, then remove them before heating the water.) Bring the water to a boil (WITHOUT the cups in the pan), and immediately reduce to lowest heat. Place the cups into the water and cover the pot with a tight fitting lid. Cook for approximately 20 minutes.

Remove from pot, remove foil and serve warm in the ramekins. Optional: serve with hot sauce.

Note: If the dish has a bit of water on top once it's cooked…that is not uncooked egg. It is simply water from the steaming process.

Serves 2

Cole Slaw

This is a rather traditional cole slaw recipe, but I included it because I make a version of it almost every Shabbos. I love the horseradish in the dish…and since Chrayn makes me think of Pesach, I eliminated the kitniyot ingredients so that I could add it to this collection.

Ingredients:

14 oz. Shredded Cabbage
(about 7 cups)

For the Dressing:
1 cup Parve Mayonnaise
¼ cup Sugar
2 Tbs. White Vinegar
2 Tbs. Prepared Horseradish
1 tsp. Onion Powder
½ tsp. Salt
½ tsp. Black Pepper

Serves 6-8

Instructions:

Combine all dressing ingredients in a small bowl. Mix well.

Cover and place in refrigerator for about an hour. This yields approximately 1½ c. of dressing.

Add about 3/4 c. (or more to taste) of the dressing to the shredded cabbage in a large bowl.

Mix well. Cover and refrigerate for about an hour before serving. The cabbage will wilt a bit so you may need less dressing than you expect.

Add more dressing to taste before serving, if desired.

Fried Plantains

PARVE

I am always searching for new vegetable side dishes. Although plantains are fruits, in many places they function a lot like vegetables. They are relatively starchy, and bring a bit of natural sweetness to a meal. Plantains are not the same as bananas, and they are not too hard to find in most areas. They get sweeter as they ripen, so the best way to make this dish is to use the ripest plantains you can find.

Ingredients:

2 Plantains
¼ -¹/₃ cup Oil
1 tsp. Paprika
½ tsp. Turmeric
Salt, to taste
Pinch of Cayenne, optional

Instructions:

Peel the plantains and slice them diagonally into pieces approximately ½" thick.

In a small bowl, combine paprika, turmeric, salt and cayenne (if using). Sprinkle some of this mixture onto one side of each slice.

Heat oil in a sturdy pan over medium high heat. Once the oil is hot, add the plantains. Work in batches if the pan is not large enough to hold them all at once. Cook for about 3-4 minutes on each side, until they are golden brown. Remove to a paper towel lined rack to drain any excess oil. Serve warm.

Serves 4-6

Chupe de Papa (Potatoes in a Creamy Tomato Sauce)

PARVE OR DAIRY

This is a unique potato dish that is a delicious side for a fleishig meal, but it is so flavorful that I've eaten it alone as a main course on a quiet night in. If you are not serving it with a meat meal, it is particularly good topped with shredded mozzarella cheese.

Ingredients:

1 Tbs. Olive Oil
2 Tbs. Margarine or Butter*
4 large Yukon Gold Potatoes (unpeeled, cut into medium sized chunks)
1 large Yellow Onion, diced
2 large Roma Tomatoes, chopped
2 cloves Garlic, minced
1 cup Coconut Milk
½ cup Broth (Be sure to use vegetable broth if you are making this parve)
1 tsp. Paprika
½ tsp. Salt (plus more to taste. I generally use almost 1 tsp. in this dish, depending on how salty the broth is.)
½ tsp. Black Pepper (plus more to taste)
1/8 - ¼ tsp. Cayenne pepper (optional)

Optional: Shredded Mozzarella

Instructions:

Heat oil over medium high heat in a sturdy pot on the stove. Add onions and sauté until translucent. (About 7-10 minutes)

Add margarine (or butter), garlic and tomato. Cook for about 5 minutes.

Add salt, black pepper and paprika and cook for another 3-5 minutes.

Add broth and coconut milk. Mix well. Add Cayenne Pepper to taste if you'd like it to have a bit of a kick.

Add potatoes and bring to a boil. Reduce to a simmer and cook, covered for about 30-40 minutes, until the potatoes are soft.

Adjust seasoning to taste.

Note: If you are making this dish dairy, sprinkle shredded mozzarella on top before serving.

*Be sure to use margarine if you are making this parve.

Serves 4-6

Sweet and Sour Carrots

PARVE

I love sweet and sour flavors together, so I am always looking for vegetables that stand up well to this combination. The natural sweetness in carrots makes them a great fit for this flavor profile. I am also always looking for uses for the imitation soy sauce I buy at Pesach, since I can never get through the entire bottle.

Ingredients:

5 large Carrots, peeled and
    sliced into long diagonal coins
2 Tbs. Oil
2 cloves Garlic, minced
$^1/_3$ cup White Wine Vinegar
¼ cup Sugar
1-2 tsp. Pesach Imitation Soy
    Sauce
Salt and Black Pepper to taste

Instructions:

Heat oil in a sauté pan over medium heat. Add carrots and cook for about 5-8 minutes. Add garlic and cook for an additional 1-2 minutes.

In a small bowl, mix vinegar, sugar and imitation soy sauce. Make sure that the sugar is well dissolved. Add this mixture to the carrots on the stove and combine thoroughly.

Add salt and pepper to taste, and allow to cook until the sauce thickens a bit and the carrots reach the desired tenderness.

Adjust seasoning to taste.

Serves 4-6

Sauteed Mushrooms

One of the most frustrating parts of planning a menu for me is choosing vegetable side dishes. This is a staple I've used for a long time because it is delicious and cooks very quickly. It also complements a wide variety of mains.

Ingredients:

1-2 Tbs. Olive Oil
1 Shallot, minced
4 cloves Garlic, minced
6 oz. White Mushrooms, chopped or sliced
5 oz. Shiitake Mushrooms, chopped or sliced
6 oz Cremini Mushrooms, chopped or sliced
5-6 sprigs Fresh Oregano
$1/3$ cup Cabernet
1 Tbs. Balsamic Vinegar
Salt and Black Pepper to taste

Instructions:

Heat oil in a pan over medium high heat. Add shallot and cook for 3-4 minutes.

Add mushrooms and cook for 6-8 minutes, until soft.

Add garlic and cook for another 2 minutes.

Add wine, oregano, vinegar, salt and pepper. Cook for 5-7 minutes.

Adjust seasoning to taste.

Serves 6

Cauliflower Rice

Cauliflower rice is really nothing more than cauliflower cut small enough to serve as a low carb (kitniyot free!) substitute for rice. During the year, the easiest way to prepare it is to simply buy it pre-chopped. However, if you do not have access to riced cauliflower during Pesach, I wanted to include this "recipe" so that you can use it as an accompaniment to any dish that would ordinarily be served with rice or some other starch. It's a great substitute to include even after Pesach ends if you want to reduce the carbs in your diet.

Ingredients:

1 head Cauliflower
½ - 1 Tbs. Olive Oil or Cooking Spray
Salt to taste

Instructions:

I prefer to use the grater attachment of a food processor to make cauliflower rice, but if you don't have one, you can use the largest holes on a box grater. If you work with a box grater, you may want to cut the cauliflower into slightly larger pieces. You may be more likely to cut your fingers if you use florets, so be careful. Make sure that the cauliflower is totally dry before grating.

Grate the cauliflower until it approximates the size of grains of rice.

It is best to cook the cauliflower rice right away. If you try to store it in the fridge, uncooked, it will start to smell and go bad quickly.

To cook, simply heat olive oil or cooking spray in a skillet on the stove over medium heat. Add the cauliflower and cook until it softens, but is not mushy.

Add salt to taste.

Serves 8-10

Buffalo Cauliflower

PARVE OR DAIRY

I don't have a high tolerance for spicy food, but with a hot sauce that has a lot of flavor without a crazy amount of heat, even I can really enjoy these vegetarian "hot wings." They can also be made by combining barbeque sauce with cayenne pepper if you cannot locate a good kosher l'Pesach hot sauce.

Ingredients:

1 head Cauliflower, cut into
  florets
2 Eggs, lightly beaten
¾ cup Potato Flour
1 tsp. Paprika
1 tsp. Garlic Powder
½ tsp. Turmeric
½ tsp. Salt
½ tsp. Black Pepper

For the Sauce:
¼ cup Margarine or Butter
¼ cup Hot Sauce
2 Tbs. Honey
1 clove Garlic, minced

Instructions:

Preheat oven to 400° F.

Line a baking sheet with parchment paper.

Combine potato flour and spices in a medium bowl. Mix well.

After checking the eggs, place them in a small bowl and lightly beat them. Dip the cauliflower florets into the beaten eggs, then coat them with the flour/spice mixture. Shake off any excess and place onto the baking sheet. Do not crowd the pieces. For a crispier result, place the cauliflower on an oven safe wire rack set on top of the baking sheet.

Bake for 20 minutes.

While the cauliflower is baking in the oven, melt the margarine in a small saucepan on the stove. Add the garlic and cook for about 2 minutes over medium high heat. Add hot sauce and honey and cook for about 5 minutes until the mixture thickens a bit. Set aside.

Remove cauliflower from the oven, but leave the oven on.

Dip each piece of cauliflower into the sauce, coating them well. Return the sauced pieces to the baking sheet and cook in the oven for another 10 minutes.

Serve hot or warm.

Serves 6

Sweets

Pesach Puff Pastry Dough

This is an incredibly versatile dough. It can be dairy or parve, based on whether you use margarine or butter. It is a great foundation for a variety of sweet and savory dishes. Several suggested uses follow. The easiest way to make the dough is to use an electric stand or hand mixer, but I tested mixing it by hand to make sure that it is possible. It takes a bit of effort, but you do not need to invest in special equipment to make this dough.

Ingredients:

½ cup Water
½ stick Margarine or Butter (Be
   sure to use margarine to
   make this parve)
½ cup Potato Flour/Starch
3 Eggs*

Instructions:

Place water and margarine or butter in a small saucepan on the stove and bring to a boil.

Add potato flour all at once and mix until it forms into a ball.

Remove from stove and cool slightly.

Transfer the dough to a mixing bowl or an electric mixer.

Add eggs one at a time, mixing well after each addition until a cohesive dough forms. If you are mixing by hand, you must mix vigorously to get the dough to form....but it will happen.

Incorporate dough into whichever recipe you are using. (See pages 179-183 for ideas, such as cream puffs, savory filled puffs, eclairs, churros, or pie crust.)

*You may prefer certain recipes with a dough that does not puff as much. For recipes like churros or pie crust, you may want a denser dough if you do not want the lightest, airiest pastry possible. For a denser result, use 2 eggs instead of 3.

Yields 1 batch of dough

Cream Puffs/Eclairs/Croquembouche   **PARVE OR DAIRY**

One of the most basic uses for the Pesach Pastry Dough (page 177) is to form it into balls or log shapes. Once they are baked and cooled, you can fill them with any sweet or savory filling. They can function as an elegant part of an appetizer, or as a versatile dessert.

Instructions:

Preheat oven to 425°F.

Form the dough into balls on a parchment lined baking sheet (roughly the size of golf balls, but any size will work) using either two spoons or a pastry bag. If you are making eclairs, pipe or form the dough into log shapes. Bake at 425°F for 15 minutes, then reduce heat to 350°F and cook for approximately 15 minutes more. If you are making balls, watch them closely, as they may need a bit less time to cook. Remove from oven and allow to cool completely before filling.

To fill the pastries, simply use a knife to create a small hole and use a pastry bag or plastic baggie with the corner cut off to squeeze in the desired filling.

The sweet filled pastries can be served plain or topped with a chocolate glaze or a dollop of whipped cream or parve frosting.

Filling Suggestions:
<u>Sweet:</u> Whipped Cream, Parve Whipped Topping, Custard, Hazelnut-Chocolate Spread, Chocolate or White Chocolate Ganache (see page 189), Lemon Curd (see page 199)

<u>Savory:</u> Salmon Mousse, Pâté, Store-bought Salatim, Herb-Goat Cheese Paste

1 batch of the puff pastry dough yields approximately 15-18 cream puffs.

Croquembouche:

One of the most impressive ways to serve cream puffs is to arrange them into a Croquembouche. This is essentially a tower of cream puffs drizzled with a simple caramel.

There are multiple ways to assemble the tower. I have seen people build a cone of construction paper or foam covered with plastic wrap and parchment paper to create a structure, but you can just build a tower of the puffs alone with no added support. I have even used toothpicks to hold each puff in place as a shortcut.

Ingredients:

Filled Cream Puffs (prepared in
  advance using instructions
  above)
2 ½ cups Sugar
½ cup Water

Instructions:

Prepare filled cream puffs and structural cone (if using one) in advance.

Mix water and sugar in a saucepan. Use a wet pastry brush or damp fingers to wipe off any sugar crystals that are stuck to the sides of the pan. Heat over a medium-high heat until the mixture begins to bubble and turn a golden brown. Do NOT stir. Once the caramel is thick, sticky and golden brown, remove from heat.   cont.

Do not allow the caramel to get too dark, or it will have a burned flavor.

This caramel will be used to hold the puffs in place, almost like an edible glue.

If you created a structural cone, place it in the center of your serving platter. Gently dip the cream puffs into the caramel and arrange them around the base of the cone or in a circle on your serving platter.

If you want to create a larger tower, begin with a bigger circle. To create a smaller tower, begin with a smaller circle.

Carefully, continue to dip the cream puffs in caramel and add layers to the structure. (I use toothpicks as needed to add stability if I don't start with a cone.) Pay attention to add caramel to the cream puffs in the areas that will touch others, in order to help them stick.

Add cream puffs in layers working in and up to create a tower that tapers to a point. There should be 1 lone cream puff at the top when you are done.

Once the structure is complete, allow the caramel to cool to the point where a fork that is inserted and lifted out will create wispy threads of sugar. Bring the saucepan near the tower and use a fork to gently drizzle these threads over and around the tower to create a thin web of crystalized caramel. You may skip this step entirely, if desired.

Chill until serving.

Note: Depending on the size of the croquembouche you are making, you will probably need between 25-50 cream puffs.

Cream Puff Pastry Pie

DAIRY OR PARVE

This is one of the easiest desserts I make. It is the dessert that I throw together if I don't have time to make anything "real." Essentially, it is just the puff pastry dough spread into a pie pan. You can fill it with anything. Mousse fillings work especially well. The recipe here is just one simple option. This is also a recipe where you may want a crust that doesn't puff quite as much. A denser, less "eggy" crust works well, so feel free to use 2 eggs instead of 3.

Ingredients:

Pesach Puff Pastry Dough
   (See Page 177)
1 packet Instant Vanilla
   Pudding
1 cup Milk or Non-Dairy
   Whipped Topping
2 cups Heavy Cream or Non-
   Dairy Whipped Topping
Fresh Fruit or Canned Fruit Pie
   Filling

Serves 8

Instructions:

Preheat oven to 425°F.

Prepare the Pesach Puff Pastry Dough. Spread the dough evenly onto a pie pan, making sure to cover the bottom and sides of the dish. It will seem thin, but the crust will puff as it bakes.

Bake for 15 minutes at 425°F, then reduce heat to 350°F and bake for another 15 minutes. Turn off the oven and let the pie crust cool inside.

Prepare the filling by mixing the instant pudding, milk and cream (or non-dairy alternative if you are making this parve) in the bowl of an electric mixer or bowl with a hand mixer. Whip until the filling has the consistency of whipped cream. Once the pie crust has cooled, pour the filling into the crust and top with fresh fruit or canned fruit filling. Chill until ready to serve.

Churros

Churros are a fun, unique dessert option. They are one of my favorite uses for Pesach Puff Pastry Dough. They are deep fried, so it is a good idea to invest in a cooking thermometer if you plan to make this recipe. You may also want a large star pastry tip and possibly a pastry bag, though they are not necessary. I always make the denser version of the pastry dough for this application, but the standard version does create a beautifully light, airy churro.

Ingredients:

Pesach Puff Pastry Dough* (See Page 177)
Cooking Oil for frying
½ cup Sugar
2 tsp. Cinnamon
½ tsp. Salt

Instructions:

*Note: This pastry dough creates a light, airy churro that puffs considerably when fried. If you'd like a denser churro, use 2 eggs instead of 3 in the dough.

Prepare Pesach Puff Pastry Dough.

Combine sugar, cinnamon and salt. Pour it onto a plate and set aside.

In a sturdy deep pot on the stove, heat oil to 365°- 380°F. It is best to use a cooking thermometer to ensure that the oil is at the correct temperature. The most common cooking oil used during Passover is cottonseed oil, which has a smoke point of 420°F, so it is a good option for this recipe. Olive oil has a lower smoke point, so it is NOT recommended.

Fit a large star tip onto a pastry bag. (Or substitute a large plastic Ziploc-type baggie with a corner cut off.) Fill the bag with the pastry dough and twist the back of the bag to keep the dough in.

Traditionally, churros are piped directly into the hot oil, but I don't like getting that close to the oil and risking potential splashing.

Lay out a piece of parchment paper on a cutting board and pipe the churros onto the parchment. The churros can be as short or long as you like. I find a 4-5" length easiest to work with. Using a spatula or silicon scraper, gently transfer the churros into the hot oil in batches. Allow plenty of room so that the individual pastries are not crowded in the oil.

Turn as needed so that each side is cooked. Once they reach the desired darkness, remove from oil with a slotted spoon and set on a cooling rack lined with paper towels. Check the temperature of the oil periodically to make sure that it doesn't cool too much between batches.

While the churros are still hot, roll them in the cinnamon/sugar mixture to coat them thoroughly. Sprinkle with extra salt, if necessary. (If you used an unsalted margarine to make the pastry dough, they might need a bit more salt, so season to taste.)

Yields about 12-14 Churros

Dark Chocolate Cookies

DAIRY OR PARVE*

My husband loves to eat rich dark chocolate, so he is a big fan of these cookies because they are really intense! I make them with 72% chocolate, but you can use a lower percentage (or even milk chocolate if making a dairy batch) to dial back the intensity.

Ingredients:

1⅛ cups Sugar
⅔ cup Tapioca Flour
¼ tsp. Baking Soda
½ tsp. Salt
3½ bars (12.25 oz) 72% Parve Dark Chocolate*
3½ Tbs. Butter or Margarine*
3 Eggs
1 tsp. White Vinegar
¼ cup Parve Chocolate Chips*
⅓ cup Chopped Pecans

*Be sure to use margarine and parve chocolate if making this recipe parve.

Instructions:

Combine sugar, tapioca flour, baking soda and salt in a large bowl. Mix well, so that there are no lumps. Set aside.

Bring a small pot of water to a simmer on the stove. This will serve as the bottom of a double boiler to melt the chocolate.

Break up the chocolate bars into pieces and put them in a heat proof (metal or silicone) bowl. Place the bowl on the simmering pot of water. Ensure that no water comes into contact with the chocolate. (Even a small amount will make the chocolate seize.) Gently stir the chocolate until it is entirely melted. (Make sure to use a pot holder to hold the bowl in place while you stir if it is metal.)

Yields about 18 cookies

Add the margarine (or butter) to the melted dark chocolate. Stir until it melts and the chocolate and margarine are well combined. Remove from heat and set aside, but do not allow to cool too much.

Lightly beat 3 whole eggs with the vinegar. Add this to the tapioca flour mixture. Whisk together until it forms a cohesive batter.

Slowly add the melted chocolate mixture to this batter. Use a rubber scraper to gently mix until well combined. (The rubber scraper helps to ensure that you get all of the batter combined with the chocolate mixture.)

Add the chocolate chips and chopped pecans and mix until just combined.

Cover the bowl with plastic wrap and put the cookie dough in the refrigerator for at least two hours to chill.

Once the dough has chilled, preheat the oven to 375° F, and line a baking sheet with parchment paper. Roll the dough into golf ball sized balls and place about 2 inches apart on the baking sheet. They will spread. Press down on the balls with your fingers to form thick discs. (I make them about ½ inch thick. The more you press, the thinner and flatter the final cookies will be.)

Bake the cookies for 9-12 minutes. Baking them for 9-10 minutes results in a cookie that is extremely gooey, and almost feels "raw". 11-12 minutes results in a dryer cookie texture.

Allow the cookies to cool on the pan for at least 8-10 minutes before moving them to a cooling rack. They will firm up a bit during this time.

Dacquoise

A dacquoise is a French dessert that was born for Pesach. It is a nut flour meringue that does not require any kind of chametz or kitniyot. The variety of desserts that you can make with this base is innumerable. The term "Dacquoise" can either refer to the meringue layer itself or the entire assembled dessert. You can make the meringues in circular or rectangular shapes and fill/frost the layers with any combination of flavors. Chocolate, caramel and coffee flavors work particularly well with this base. You can simply add a filling (mousse, ganache, whipped topping, etc.) between and on top of the meringue layers and allow them to show, or cover the entire thing with a glaze or frosting so that it looks like a more traditional layered cake. As the frosting sits on the meringues, they soften, so don't worry if the meringue layers seem dry/hard after you bake them. I have even seen people use a dacquoise as the base for an entrement...if you really want to put in a lot of work and have the freezer space!

Ingredients:

6 Egg Whites, room temperature
1½ cups Superfine (Baker's) Sugar
½ tsp. White Vinegar
¼ tsp. Salt
¾ cup Almond Flour
½ cup Hazelnut Flour

Instructions:

Preheat oven to 325°F.

Bring a small or medium pot of water to a low boil on the stove. This will serve as the bottom of a double boiler.

In the metal bowl of an electric stand mixer (or a heat-proof bowl to use with an electric hand mixer), whisk together the egg whites, sugar, vinegar and salt. Place the bowl over the pot on the stove to heat as you continue to whisk vigorously. I highly recommend using a French whisk for this. You should use a pot holder or silicone glove to protect your hand while holding the bowl in place.

Continue whisking until the mixture is very foamy and begins to thicken. It should reach a temperature of at least 165°F. If you do not have a thermometer, you can rub some of the egg white between your fingers. It should be totally smooth and there should be no grit from the sugar.

Remove from heat and return the bowl to the stand of the mixer (or to a counter where you can use an electric hand mixer). Using a whisk attachment, whip the mixture until it just reaches stiff peaks.

Thoroughly combine the almond and hazelnut flours in a bowl, then gently fold them into the egg white mixture using a rubber scraper or large spoon.

On parchment lined baking sheets, spread the batter into 3 circles or rectangles. You can draw the shapes under the parchment if you need a guide so that they will be roughly the same size. The batter does not spread too much during baking, so you do not need excessive space between meringues if you bake more than one on the same sheet. You can also make the meringues into smaller shapes to create individual desserts.

Bake for 30 minutes. Allow the meringues to cool completely in the oven before removing them. When you remove them from the oven, it is fine to allow them to sit and dry out even more. They may seem hard and dry, but the fillings will soften them.

Spread or pipe frosting, ganache, mousse, curd, jam, whipped topping or any desired filling between and on top of the meringue layers. Since a dacquoise is very sweet, fillings that are unsweetened and add some tartness work well. Chill until serving.

Serves 8-10

Pictured with Parve Buttercream Frosting and Simple Ganache

Parve Buttercream Frosting

This frosting is a Swiss meringue style buttercream. You can use it to frost or fill cakes, pavlovas or cream puffs or add to any dessert that needs a sweet creamy layer. I started using Swiss meringue as a base for my pavlova because it adds stability. But I realized that this technique also works for this frosting, and it eliminates the need for powdered sugar, which is a component of traditional buttercream that is not kosher for Pesach. I also recommend using a French whisk for this, and any other meringue recipes.

Ingredients:

6 Egg Whites, room temperature
1¾ cups Superfine Sugar*
½ tsp. White Vinegar
1½ cups Margarine (You can use butter if you are making a dairy frosting)
Pinch of Salt

Instructions:

Bring some water to a boil in a small pot on the stove. Reduce to a simmer. This will serve as the bottom of a double boiler.

If you have an electric stand mixer, remove the bowl to make the meringue on the stove. If you will be using an electric hand mixer, use a heat proof bowl. Place egg whites, sugar and vinegar in the bowl. Whisk together using a French whisk. Once the ingredients are well combined, place the bowl over the pot on the stove. Continue whisking as the mixture heats. Use a pot holder or silicone glove to protect your hand while holding the bowl in place.

Whisk vigorously as the mixture gets frothy. It should reach a temperature of about 165°F before you remove it from the stove.

If you don't have a candy thermometer, rub some of the egg whites between your fingers. If it is totally smooth and you don't feel any grit from the sugar, it is done. By this point, the mixture should be very frothy, especially if you are using a French whisk.

Remove from heat and return to the base of the stand mixer. (Or use an electric hand mixer). Whisk on high until the egg whites form stiff peaks.

When the egg whites reach this stage, the bowl should be cooled off considerably. The key to this recipe is for the margarine to be about the same temperature as the egg white mixture. If necessary, chill the egg whites in the refridgerator. Once the egg whites are cool, add margarine.

Using a paddle attachment, add the margarine 1 tablespoon at a time. Mix on a medium or low speed and make sure that each tablespoon is fully incorporated before adding the next one. Once all of the margarine is mixed in, add a pinch of salt and mix until well combined.

If the frosting is not coming together, place the bowl in the fridge for 10-15 minutes to chill, then continue mixing.

*It is possible to use regular granulated sugar, but there are great superfine (Baker's) sugars that are kosher for Pesach. I find that the superfine sugar is easier to work with in meringues.

Yields about 5 cups

Pictured with Dacquoise

Simple Ganache

This is my go-to, easy option for any creamy filling. I use it in all kinds of layered desserts, cream puffs and cakes. Anytime something could benefit from a chocolate or white chocolate mousse, I substitute this. If you are making a parve dessert, simply use a parve non-dairy whipped topping in place of the whipped cream, and be sure to select chips that are parve.

Ingredients:

- 2 cups Heavy Cream (Or parve non-dairy whipping cream substitute)
- 8 oz. Chocolate Bar or Chips* (Use milk chocolate, dark chocolate or white chocolate, depending on your taste. Be sure to use Parve chips if making this recipe parve.)

Instructions:

Place the chocolate chips in a heat proof bowl.

In a saucepan on the stove, bring the cream to a boil. Pour the hot cream over the chocolate chips and mix well so that they melt entirely.

Strain the mixture into a bowl and chill in the refrigerator overnight or until the mixture is completely cold.

Transfer the chilled mixture to the bowl of an electric stand mixer or a bowl for use with a hand mixer. With a whisk attachment, whip the mixture until it has a stiff mousse-like consistency.

*Chocolate chips often include additional ingredients, so if you use a chocolate bar the flavor of the ganache will be better.

Yields about 2 ½ cups

Pictured with Dacquoise

Cheesecake Cups

This is another old family recipe that just happened to be chametz free. It is a great, easy dessert that is always a crowd pleaser. It's also a great addition to a dairy brunch. You can use any kind of fresh or canned fruit toppings or curd.

Ingredients:

3 (8oz.) packages Cream Cheese
   (softened to room temperature)
5 Eggs
1 cup Sugar
½ tsp. Vanilla

For the Filling:
1 cup Sour Cream
½ tsp. Vanilla
¼ cup Sugar

For the Topping:
Cherry or Blueberry Pie Filling,
   Fresh Fruit or Citrus Curd

Cupcake Liners for baking

Instructions:

Preheat oven to 300°F.

Beat the softened cream cheese until smooth.

Add eggs one at a time and mix until a smooth batter forms. (This takes longer than you'd think.)

Add sugar and vanilla and mix until well combined.

Line a muffin pan with cupcake liners. Pour the batter into the liners until they are about ¾ full.

Bake for 40 minutes. Remove from oven and allow to cool in the pan until a dip forms in the center of each cup.

In a small bowl, combine the filling ingredients. (sour cream, vanilla and sugar)

Spoon some of the filling into each cup. The filling should not overflow.

Return the pan to the oven and cook for another 5-8 minutes.

Remove from oven and allow to cool.

Refrigerate.

Add fruit topping before serving.

Yields about 24 cheesecake cups

Chocolate Soufflé

I always make soufflés in individual ramekins, but they can be made in a large soufflé dish. These do fall a bit as they cool, so it's best to serve warm straight out of the oven. But even if they fall, they still taste wonderful. They can be served in ramekins or be popped out and plated. I use dark chocolate in this recipe and it results in a very rich soufflé. You may substitute dark chocolate with a lower percentage of cacao, or even milk chocolate if you are making a dairy meal. The two pieces of slightly specialized equipment I use for this recipe are a silicon rubber scraper and a French whisk. I love to use a silicon scraper for melting chocolate and folding meringues. The shape of a French whisk really does help to get more air into a mixture. It is easy to find cheap versions of each that work really well, but of course, they are not absolutely necessary.

Ingredients:

7 oz. (2 bars) 72% Parve Dark
   Chocolate
4 Tbs. Sugar (plus a bit extra for
   the baking dishes)
¼ cup Butter or Margarine*
   (plus a bit extra for the baking
   dishes)
2 tsp. Vanilla
4 Egg Yolks
5 Egg Whites
1 tsp. White Vinegar
pinch of Salt (about ⅛ tsp.)

Instructions:

Bring some water to a boil in a small pot on the stove. Reduce to a simmer. This will serve as the bottom of a double boiler.

Place margarine and chocolate in a metal or heat proof glass bowl and set it over the pot of simmering water. Melt the chocolate and margarine, mixing until smooth and well combined. Do not allow any water to get into the bowl or the chocolate will seize up.

Remove from heat.

In a separate bowl, whisk together yolks, vanilla and salt. Add this to the melted chocolate mixture. Mix well.

Place egg whites and vinegar in the bowl of an electric stand mixer (or a bowl to use with an electric hand mixer), and whisk until foamy. Once they are foamy, add sugar and whisk until stiff peaks form.

One of the most important steps in a soufflé is combining these two mixtures while retaining as much of the air from the egg whites as possible.

Add 1/3 of the egg white mixture to the chocolate mixture. Gently combine. (It is easiest to do this gently with a silicon or rubber scraper.)

Fold in another 1/3 of the egg white mixture to this and carefully combine.

Gently fold the remaining 1/3 of the egg whites into the chocolate mixture. Cover and refrigerate for at least 15 minutes.

While the batter is cooling in the refrigerator, preheat the oven to 375°F and prepare the ramekins.

Grease the inside of each ramekin with either butter or margarine. (Make sure to use margarine if you are making this parve.) Add sugar to each dish and tilt to coat the bottom and sides entirely. The texture of the sugar on the sides of the dish will help the soufflé rise properly. Take a paper towel or cloth and wipe any grease/sugar from the top edge of the dish down to the inner ridge.

Remove batter from the refrigerator and fill each ramekin up to the first inner ridge.

Place all of the ramekins on a baking sheet and place baking sheet in the oven.

Immediately after placing the soufflés into the oven, decrease heat to 350°F. Bake for 18-20 minutes. Do NOT open the oven door to check on them. (If using a large soufflé dish, rather than individual ramekins, cook for 35-37 minutes.)

As soon as they are removed from the oven, they will begin to fall as they cool. Serve immediately.

Option: serve with berry compote, jam or whipped topping

*Be sure to use parve margarine if making this recipe parve.

Yield: 6 (7 oz.) ramekins

Hazelnut Chocolate Chip Cookies

PARVE OR DAIRY

These cookies have a great texture that really feels different from most Pesach desserts. If you have an electric mixer, of course that'll make it easier, but I've made them totally by hand many times. They are VERY fragile when they come out of the oven. They will firm up as they cool, so allow them to sit on the pan for a while before moving them to a rack. I usually line the baking sheet with parchment paper, and that allows me to pull the entire batch of cookies onto a cooling rack before they firm up completely. You can also use these as the crumble base for a layered dessert.

Ingredients:

1 stick Margarine or Butter*
½ cup Sugar
1 Egg
¼ cup Hazelnut Butter
1 tsp. Vanilla
1 cup plus 3 Tbs Hazelnut Flour
2 Tbs. Coconut Flour
¼ tsp. Salt
½ tsp. Baking Soda
½ cup Chocolate Chips*
$^1/_3$ cup Hazelnuts, roughly
   chopped

Instructions:

Preheat oven to 350°F. Line a baking sheet with parchment paper.

In a mixing bowl, cream together margarine (or butter), sugar and egg.

Add hazelnut butter and vanilla and mix well.

In a separate bowl, combine hazelnut flour, coconut flour, salt and baking soda. Mix well so that there are no clumps.

Add this dry mixture to the margarine/sugar/egg mixture and mix until well combined.

Stir in chocolate chips and chopped hazelnuts.

Use two spoons to scoop out batter and form it into balls on the baking sheet. The cookies spread, so leave plenty of room between them.

Optional: Place the baking sheet with the cookie dough balls into the fridge for 20 minutes before baking. This is more important if you are using butter for dairy cookies. Chilling them first will keep them from flattening too much. Parve cookies made with margarine tend to hold their shape a bit more, even without pre-chilling.

Bake cookies for 12-14 minutes.

The cookies are very fragile when they come out of the oven, so allow them to cool a bit before removing them from the baking sheet. They firm up as they cool.

*Be sure to use margarine and parve chocolate chips if you are making this recipe parve.

Yields 22-24 cookies

Mini Lemon Meringue Cookies

PARVE

These little meringues can be served alone as a light dessert, or they can be a part of a beautiful, more elaborate treat. I like to serve them as a layer or topping in a dish with fruit, lemon curd and non-dairy whipped "cream." You can also experiment with different flavors. Peppermint is particularly good if you can track down a peppermint extract that is kosher for Pesach. It is also important to use superfine or "Baker's" sugar in this recipe. It is easy to find certified superfine sugar online, and it makes a big difference.

Ingredients:

2 Egg Whites
½ cup Superfine Sugar
2 Tbs. Lemon Juice

Instructions:

Preheat oven to 200°F.

Bring a pot of water to a low boil on the stove. This will serve as the bottom of a double boiler.

If you have an electric stand mixer, use the bowl as the top of your double boiler. If you will be using a hand mixer, use any metal or heat proof bowl.

Place egg whites and sugar into the bowl and place over the boiling water. Reduce the heat a bit, but maintain at least a simmer. You will need some kind of pot holder or heat proof glove to hold the bowl in place as you whisk.

Whisk the egg/sugar mixture by hand over the double boiler until the sugar is completely dissolved and the mixture is smooth. (If you rub a bit of the egg white between your fingers, you shouldn't feel any grittiness from the sugar.)

Remove from heat and continue whisking using either an electric hand mixer or a stand mixer. Whisk until the egg whites reach a soft peak stage.

Add lemon juice and whisk for 1-2 more minutes. The end result should be just short of stiff peaks.

Line a baking sheet with parchment paper. Use a pastry bag or large zip-top baggie with a corner cut off to pipe the meringues onto the baking sheet.

Bake for approximately 80 minutes. Allow to cool before attempting to remove them from the parchment.

Yields approximately 100 small cookies

Lemon (or Lime) Curd

I use a lot of egg whites, so I always have extra yolks around. Lemon (or really, any citrus) curd is a great way to use them up. This delectable, sweet and sour topping can work with numerous desserts, or even be served totally alone. Serve with fruit, on pavlova, as a filling for cakes or cream puffs…or any number of other ways.

Ingredients:

2 Whole Eggs
2 Egg Yolks
½ cup Sugar
zest of 2 Lemons (about 2 Tbs.)
½ cup Lemon Juice
6 Tbs. Margarine or Butter*
pinch of Salt (optional, but
    a good idea if you are using
    unsalted margarine or butter)

Instructions:

Combine all ingredients, except margarine/ butter in a sauce pan. Whisk together over medium heat for 2-3 minutes. (*Note: some people are sensitive to the metallic flavor that lemon can pick up from a metal bowl or pan. To avoid this, use a heat proof glass bowl over a simmering pot of water instead of heating directly.)

Cut the margarine/butter into 4 to 6 pieces and carefully add this to the lemon/egg mixture on the stove. Whisk for another 10-12 minutes until the curd thickens. Do NOT allow to boil.

Remove from heat. The curd will continue to thicken as it cools. Pour into a heat proof bowl and cover with plastic wrap directly on the surface of the curd to avoid forming a tough skin. Refrigerate until using. This dish should last for up to a week in the refrigerator.

Serve with fruit or any desserts that pair well with lemon flavor. It goes especially well on a pavlova. I also love this curd over fruit, topped with mini meringue cookies (see page 196).

Note: substitute lime, grapefruit or any citrus in place of the lemon juice/zest for a different flavor.

*Be sure to use margarine when making this recipe parve.

Yield: about 1 ½ cups

Pavlova

This may be my all-time favorite dessert for Pesach. It is incredibly versatile and delicious. Pavlovas can be tricky, and it took me months of experimenting and dozens upon dozens of flawed attempts to finally create a reliable method for this dreamy dessert. It is essentially a meringue base covered with anything you like. Traditionally, it is covered in whipped cream and fruit, but there are countless options. Pavlovas are very sweet, so using a topping that has some tartness is a great option. I like to use a lemon or lime curd with fruit on top. You can also cover it in caramel, hazelnut-chocolate spread, mousse/ganache or anything you like. The base is made the night before and cools/dries overnight in the oven, so this is a good option for a Shabbos lunch if you prepare the toppings in advance. The one thing to note while working with meringues is that a very humid environment doesn't help. My method is relatively forgiving, but this is not a dessert to make on a rainy day. I highly recommend using a French whisk for this dish.

Ingredients:

6 Egg Whites
1½ cups Superfine Sugar
1½ tsp. Tapioca Flour
1½ tsp. White Wine Vinegar

Instructions:

Preheat oven to 300°F.

Bring a small or medium pot of water to a low boil on the stove. This will serve as the bottom of a double boiler.

In the metal bowl of an electric stand mixer (or a heat-proof bowl to use with an electric hand mixer), whisk together the egg whites and sugar. A French whisk is best for this.

Place the bowl over the pot on the stove to heat as you continue to whisk vigorously. You should use a pot holder or silicone glove to protect your hand while holding the bowl in place.

Continue whisking until the mixture is very foamy and begins to thicken. It should reach a temperature of at least 165°F. If you do not have a thermometer, you can rub some of the egg white between your fingers. It should be totally smooth and there should be no grit from the sugar.

Remove from heat and return the bowl to the stand of the mixer (or to a counter where you can use an electric hand mixer). Using a whisk attachment, whip the mixture until it just reaches stiff peaks.

In a small bowl, combine tapioca flour and vinegar to create a slurry. Mix well so that the slurry has no lumps.

Add this to the egg whites and mix for another 30-60 seconds, until the slurry is well incorporated and the egg whites are glossy and stiff.

Line a baking sheet with parchment paper and pour the egg white batter onto the center of the sheet. While maintaining as much volume as possible, use a spatula to shape the pile of batter into a circle 8-10 inches in diameter with a flat(ish) top.

Place the pavlova in the oven and immediately lower the temperature to 245°F. Bake for 90 minutes, then turn the oven off. Do NOT remove the pavlova from the oven at this point. Allow it to cool and continue drying in the oven overnight. (Or at least until it is completely cool)

Before serving, cover the pavlova with your desired toppings. (Unsweetened whipped cream or non-dairy topping with fruit, lemon curd, caramel sauce, etc.)

Note: The result should be a cohesive marshmallow-like core covered in a crisp outer meringue layer. If there is a lot of space between the inner core and the outer shell, it is a failed pavlova. If you notice a lot of liquid seeping out, that means that the sugar was not well incorporated. Using the Swiss meringue method outlined above should prevent this, but if your pavlova isn't perfect, it will still taste great. Just cover it with your toppings and no one will notice slight imperfections.

Serves 8-10

Chocolate Cake

When I began trying to make Pesach desserts, I found myself constantly whipping egg whites and yolks separately and folding them together with various ingredients. This is a staple of Pesach baking. It is crucial to get as much air as possible into baked goods, since none of the traditional leavening agents can be used. But one day, after a number of failed attempts at a cake, I gave up on separating whites and yolks out of pure frustration. I thought: "what if I just whip whole eggs really hard?" Strangely, I ended up with the best Pesach chocolate cake I had ever tried. I modified it a bit and came up with something remarkable. This is a base that can be used to make any kind of chocolate cake. Use it to make a Black Forest Cake, a German Chocolate Cake (see recipe on the following page) or use any filling and frosting to make the layered chocolate cake of your dreams. (see parve buttercream frosting recipe on page 188)

This recipe yields one layer for a 9-inch cake. I bake each cake separately during Pesach because I only have one kosher l'Pesach 9-inch pan. To make a 2 or 3 layered cake, just double or triple the recipe. If you are using an 8" pan, the layer will be a bit thicker, so increase the baking time, as needed.

Ingredients:

3 Eggs
5 Tbs. Sugar
1 tsp. White Vinegar
2 Tbs. Water
¼ tsp. Instant Coffee
½ tsp. Vanilla
¼ tsp. Salt
¼ cup Oil*
¼ cup Cocoa Powder
³⁄₈ cup Tapioca Flour
½ tsp. Baking Soda

*You may use only 2 Tbs. of oil in the recipe for a lighter, airier result. However, the cake will also be drier, so you will need to add toppings to add moisture.

Yields 1 9" layer

Instructions:

Preheat oven to 350°F. Grease a 9" cake pan and line the bottom with parchment paper.

In a small bowl, combine cocoa powder, tapioca flour, baking soda and salt. Mix thoroughly. Set aside.

Use the whisk attachment of an electric stand mixer or a hand mixer to beat the eggs and vinegar together. Add the sugar and beat on high until the mixture is significantly increased in volume and holds its form. (about 4-6 minutes)

Dissolve the instant coffee into the water and add it, along with the vanilla, to the egg mixture. Beat on high until well combined.

Gently drizzle in the oil and mix well.

Slowly add the dry ingredients to the egg mixture, mixing on a very low speed until just combined.

Pour the batter into the prepared pan and bake for 23-25 minutes.

Bake additional layers, as needed. Fill and frost the cake as desired. You can also cut up the cake into chunks and serve it as a trifle or layered dessert. It works especially well as the base for the Chocolate Cherry Napoleon on page 208.

German Chocolate Frosting

PARVE

This is a traditional German Chocolate frosting that goes well with the chocolate cake recipe in this book. It specifically calls for unsweetened coconut, so you may need to decrease the sugar if only sweetened coconut is available in your area at Pesach.

Ingredients:

½ cup Brown Sugar
½ cup Sugar
½ cup Margarine
3 Egg Yolks
1 cup Coconut Cream
1 Tbs. Vanilla
¾ cup Pecans, chopped
1 cup Unsweetened Shredded
    Coconut

Instructions:

Melt the margarine in a saucepan on the stove over medium low heat.

Whisk in brown sugar, sugar, egg yolks, vanilla and coconut cream. Bring to a low boil. Reduce heat and simmer until it thickens.

Remove from heat and mix in pecans and shredded coconut.

Allow to cool completely before frosting cake.

Yields approximately 2¼ cups

Brownies

These brownies are a delicious dessert that can be served alone or with any number of toppings...ice cream, caramel sauce, non-dairy whipped topping, fruit, etc. They could also be crumbled into a trifle or layered dessert, so there are plenty of options. This recipe works best with an 8" square brownie pan. I made it once in a 9" pan, and the brownies tasted fine, but they were a bit too flat. It is also crucial to include the walnuts. A lot of brownie recipes have nuts as an optional ingredient, but for these, the walnuts make the dish.

Ingredients:

½ cup Butter or Margarine*, melted
$^1/_3$ cup Cocoa Powder
¼ cup Brown Sugar
¼ cup Sugar
1½ tsp. Vanilla
2 Eggs, lightly beaten
1½ cup Almond Flour
½ cup Walnuts, chopped
½ tsp Salt

Instructions:

Preheat oven to 350°F.

Combine melted butter, cocoa powder, brown sugar and sugar in a bowl and mix thoroughly.

Add vanilla and eggs and mix until well combined.

Add almond flour and salt and mix until the batter is uniform.

Fold in walnuts.

Grease a square 8" pan and line it with parchment paper. Pour batter into pan and bake for 30-35 minutes.

*Be sure to use margarine to make this parve.

Makes 9-12 brownies

Coconut Cake

I was making an angel food cake for Pesach, and it was pretty good, but it felt a bit too light. So, I added some coconut flour to give it more density. The result was no longer anything like an angel food cake, but the texture was surprisingly good. This cake base can be frosted with a simple whipped cream or non-dairy whipped topping, or layered with caramel or parve buttercream. It also works great as a base for a layered dessert like a trifle. Simply cut it into pieces and layer with fruit (pineapple works great!), custard or curd and whipped topping. Since this was born out of an angel food cake recipe, I do recommend using a tube cake pan or a bundt pan. These pans will allow the cake to rise properly.

Ingredients

1 cup Tapioca Flour
½ cup Coconut Flour
½-¾ tsp. Salt
½ cup Sugar
10 Eggs, separated (room temperature)
½ cup Water
2 tsp. Vanilla
3 tsp. White Vinegar

Instructions:

Preheat oven to 325°F.

Combine tapioca flour, coconut flour and salt in a bowl and mix thoroughly. Set aside.

Lightly beat egg yolks in a small bowl. Add ½ cup water and whisk to combine. Add this to the tapioca flour mixture and mix until thoroughly combined.

Place the egg whites in the bowl of an electric stand mixer or a bowl for use with an electric hand mixer. Whip them until they are a bit foamy. Add the vinegar and whip for another minute. Add sugar and vanilla and whip to stiff peaks.

Fold about half of the egg whites into the yolk/flour mixture to lighten it a bit. Then, gently fold this mixture into the remaining egg white mixture until you have a cohesive batter. Try to maintain as much volume as possible.

Pour batter into an ungreased tube cake pan and bake for 50-60 minutes.

Invert the pan to cool. Do not remove the cake until it is completely cool. If you gently slide a table knife along the edges and push gently on the base (on top when inverted), the cake should slide out fairly easily.

Fill and frost, or, cut up the cake to make a layered dessert with your favorite toppings. This works particularly well with a caramel filling.

Serves 8-10

Chocolate Cherry Napoleon

PARVE

This recipe is for a chocolate meringue based napoleon. If you do not like the excessive sweetness or texture of a meringue, you can use the chocolate cake recipe on page 202 as the base of this dessert. If you opt for the meringue, it can also be made as a flat, sheet pan sized layer that can be filled with whipped topping and cherries and rolled into a Swiss Roll style dessert.

Ingredients:

5 Egg Whites
1 tsp. White Vinegar
½ tsp. Salt
1½ cups Superfine Sugar
$^1/_3$ cup Cocoa Powder
¾ cup Unsweetened Shredded Coconut (optional)
1 cup Brandy
1 cup Cherries, pitted and chopped
2 cups Parve Whipped Topping (or whipped cream if serving with a dairy meal)
Parve Dark Chocolate Bar, shaved into strips with a vegetable peeler or microplane

Instructions:

Preheat oven to 325°F.

Place the cherries in a bowl with the brandy and set aside.

Whip the egg whites, vinegar and salt until they are nearly at a soft peak stage.

Add the sugar and continue to beat until the mixture is very thick.

Gently fold in the cocoa powder and shredded coconut (if using).

Line a baking sheet with foil and parchment paper. Spoon the batter onto the baking sheet forming circles (or squares) that are approximately 3" in diameter and approximately ¼" thick. Bake for 30 minutes.

Remove from oven and allow to cool.

Once the meringues are cool, assemble the desserts.

Place one meringue on the bottom and cover it with a layer of whipped topping. Drain the cherries and sprinkle some onto the whipped topping.

Place another meringue on top. Cover this with additional whipped topping and top with cherries and chocolate shavings.

Serves 4-6

Index

About the Author

Ashira Ungar hosted *The Kosher Convert* YouTube series and loves travel, film and weight lifting. She has studied psychology, chemistry, medicine and business, and is always exlporing ways to make Kosher cuisine more fun and interesting. She's a wanna-be surfer girl who lives in Los Angeles...so naturally, she also does yoga.

Made in the USA
Las Vegas, NV
18 March 2025

19794432R00122